Desserts

BLOOMSBURY KITCHEN LIBRARY

Desserts

Bloomsbury Books
London

Freezing Sorbets and Ice Creams

Three freezing methods can be used. Make sure that the dessert mixture is well chilled before you freeze it.

Hand-whisking method

Place the dessert mixture in a freezer, whisk it from time to time as it firms up to break the ice crystals and aerate the mixture. Turn your freezer to its coldest setting. Use a large metal bowl, or resort to metal ice-cube trays. Place the bowl in the freezer. When a ring of crystals about 1 cm ($^1/_2$ inch) wide has formed round the outside edge of the mixture (1 to 2 hours) whisk. Return the bowl to the freezer and allow another ring to form and whisk again. Repeat until the dessert is frozen through. Allow to freeze an additional 15 minutes, then serve.

Food processor method

This method utilizes a food processor once the dessert mixture has set. Freeze in a metal bowl; when solidified—the centre may still be soft—break it into chunks and place them in a food processor. (Return the empty bowl to the freezer; you will need it later.) Process the chunks until the dessert has a smooth consistency; do not over-process or it will melt. Return to the chilled bowl and let it sit in the freezer for another 15 minutes until it firms up.

Churning method

This utilises electric and other convenience models, some containing coolants which operate in the same way as hand cranking machines. In using them, be sure to follow the manufacture's instructions carefully.

This edition published 1994 by Bloomsbury Books,
an imprint of The Godfrey Cave Group,
42 Bloomsbury Street, London, WC1B 3QJ.

ISBN 1 85471 532 1

Printed and bound in Great Britain.

Contents

Orange Slices Macerated in Red Wine and Port

Serves 8

Working time: about 20 minutes

Total time: about 2 hours and 20 minutes (includes chilling)

Calories 145
Protein 2g
Cholesterol 0mg
Total fat 1g
Saturated fat 1g
Sodium 2mg

	large oranges	6	⅛ tsp	grond cardamom or allspice	⅛ tsp
litre	Beaujolais or other fruity red wine	8 fl oz	6 tbsp	ruby port	6 tbsp
tbsp	sugar	4 tbsp	2 tbsp	currants	2 tbsp
	cinnamon stick	1	2 tbsp	toasted shredded coconut	2 tbsp

With a vegetable peeler, pare the rind from one of the oranges. Put the rind into a small saucepan with the wine, sugar, cinnamon stick, and cardamom or allspice. Bring the mixture to the boil and cook it over medium-high heat until the liquid is reduced to about 15 cl (¼ pint) – approximately 5 minutes. Remove the pan from the heat; stir in the port and currants, and set the sauce aside.

Cut away the skins, removing all the white pith, and slice the oranges into 5 mm (¼ inch) thick rounds. Arrange the orange rounds on a serving dish and pour the wine sauce over them; remove and discard the cinnamon stick. Refrigerate the dish, covered, for 2 hours.

Just before serving the oranges, sprinkle the toasted coconut over all.

Editor's Note: To toast the shredded coconut, spread it on a baking sheet and cook it in a preheated 170°C (325°F or Mark 3) oven, stirring it every 5 minutes until it has browned – about 15 minutes in all.

Poached Apricots in Caramel-Orange Sauce

Serves 8

Working time: about 45 minutes

Total time: about 2 hours and 45 minutes (includes chilling)

Calories 135

Protein 1g

Cholesterol 11mg

Total fat 3g

Saturated fat 2g

Sodium 4mg

8	large ripe apricots, or 16 small ripe apricots	8
2.5 cm	length of vanilla pod	1 inch
¼ litre	dry white wine	8 fl oz
200 g	sugar	7 oz
10 cm	strip of orange rind, 2.5 cm (1 inch) wide	4 inch

	fresh mint leaves for garnish	
	Caramel-Orange Sauce	
100 g	sugar	3½ c
1 tsp	fresh lemon juice	1 ts
12.5 cl	fresh orange juice	4 fl c
4 tbsp	double cream	4 tbs

Blanch the apricots in boiling water for 10 seconds, then plunge in iced water to arrest their cooking. Peel the apricots as soon as cool enough to handle. Cut open the groove in each apricot, splitting the flesh just enough to remove the stones. Press the edges of the apricots closed.

Slit the piece of vanilla pod lengthwise. In a heavy-bottomed saucepan set over medium heat, combine the vanilla pod with ¼ litre (8 fl oz) of water, the wine, sugar and orange rind. Bring the mixture to the boil, then reduce the heat, and simmer the syrup for 5 minutes.

Reduce the heat so that the surface of the syrup barely trembles. Add the apricots and poach, covered, until just tender – 3 to 4 minutes. Transfer

them to a plate; discard the syrup. Chill th apricots, covered, for 2 hours.

Meanwhile, prepare the sauce. In a sma saucepan, combine the sugar with the lemo juice and 3 tablespoons of water. Bring to th boil and simmer it until it turns amber – 5 to minutes. Immediately remove the pan from th heat. Slowly pour in the orange juice, then th cream. Return the pan to a low heat and simme the sauce, stirring, until it thickens slightly about 5 minutes. Transfer to a bowl, cover ar refrigerate.

Serve chilled apricots and sauce on individu: plates with a mint leaf garnish.

Orange-Banana Flowers with Caramel Sauce

Serves 6

Working time: about 25 minutes

Total time: about 40 minutes

Calories 260

Protein 2g

Cholesterol 0mg

Total fat 1g

Saturated fat 0g

Sodium 1mg

| 0 g | sugar | 7 oz | 2 | large ripe bananas | 2 |
| | oranges | 6 | ½ | lemon | ½ |

a small, heavy saucepan, combine the sugar ith 6 tablespoons of water. Bring the mixture the boil and cook it until it turns a reddish mber. Immediately remove the pan from the eat. Standing well back to avoid being splattered, owly and carefully pour in 4 tablespoons of ater. Return the pan to the heat and simmer the uce, stirring constantly, for 1 minute. Transfer e caramel sauce to the refrigerator to cool.

While the sauce is cooling, peel and segment e oranges. Peel the bananas and slice them agonally into pieces about 3 mm (⅛ inch) ick. Squeeze the lemon over the banana slices, en toss the slices to coat them with the lemon ice.

To assemble the dessert, arrange five orange segments in a circle on a plate. Place a banana slice over each of the five points where these segments meet. Arrange three orange segments in a loose circle inside the first circle, and place a banana slice over each of the three points where these segments meet. Top the assembly with two orange segments. Quarter a banana slice and arrange the quarters on top of the last two orange segments. Assemble five more orange banana flowers in the same way.

Just before serving the flowers, pour a little caramel sauce around the outside of each one, letting some of the sauce fall on to the petals.

Papayas and Melon in Sweet Chili Sauce

Serves 8

Working time: about 30 minutes

Total time: about 1 hour and 30 minutes (includes chilling)

Calories 155

Protein 1g

Cholesterol 0mg

Total fat 0g

Saturated fat 0g

Sodium 8mg

1	hot green chili pepper, halved lengthwise and seeded	**1**
12.5 cl	fresh lemon juice	**4 fl oz**

200 g	sugar	**7 o**
2	papayas	
1	cantaloupe or other melon	

Combine the chili pepper, lemon juice, sugar and ¼ litre (8 fl oz) of water in a heavy-bottomed saucepan. Bring the mixture to the boil and cook it until it has reduced to about ¼ litre (8 fl oz) of syrup. Remove the chili pepper and set the syrup aside to cool.

Seed and skin the papayas and the melon. Cut the papaya into sticks about 4 cm (1½ inches) long and 5 mm (¼ inch) square. Cut the melo into 1 cm (½ inch) cubes. Mix the fruit with th cooled syrup and chill the mixture for at lea 1 hour before serving.

Editor's Note: Chili pepper adds spark to th dessert.

Fresh Fruit in Ginger Syrup

Serves 6

Working time: about 25 minutes

Total time: about 2 hours and 30 minutes (includes chilling)

Calories 150

Protein 1g

Cholesterol 0mg

Total fat 0g

Saturated fat 0g

Sodium 3mg

1	tart green apple, quartered, cored and cut into 1 cm (½ inch) pieces	1
2	ripe peaches or nectarines, halved, stoned and cut into 1 cm (½ inch) pieces	2
1	pear, peeled, cored and cut into 1 cm (½ inch) pieces	1

225 g	blueberries, picked over and stemmed	**7½ oz**
3 tbsp	fresh lemon juice	**3 tbsp**
2 tbsp	julienned orange rind	**2 tbsp**
5 cm	ginger root, cut into 5 mm (¼ inch) rounds	**2 inch**
135 g	sugar	**4½ oz**

Place the apple, peaches, pear and blueberries in a large bowl. Pour the lemon juice over the fruit and toss well, then refrigerate the bowl.

Pour 1 litre (1¾ pints) of water into a large, heavy-bottomed saucepan over medium-high heat. Add the orange rind, ginger and sugar, and bring the mixture to the boil. Reduce the heat to medium and simmer the liquid until it is reduced to about ½ litre (16 fl oz) of syrup. Remove the ginger with a slotted spoon and discard it.

Pour the syrup into a large bowl and let it stand at room temperature for about 10 minutes. Add the fruit to the syrup and stir gently to coat the fruit. Refrigerate the dessert, covered, until the fruit is thoroughly chilled – about 1½ hours.

Editor's Note: If blueberries are not available, bilberries, stoned cherries or seedless grapes may be used instead.

Fig Flowers with Cassis Sauce

Serves 6

Working time: about 25 minutes

Total time: about 1 hour (includes chilling)

Calories 155

Protein 1g

Cholesterol 0mg

Total fat 0g

Saturated fat 0g

Sodium 5mg

½ litre	dry white wine	16 fl oz	12	fresh figs	12
1 tbsp	sugar	1 tbsp		fresh mint leaves for garnish	
4 tbsp	crème de cassis	4 tbsp			

Combine the wine and sugar in a saucepan over medium-high heat. Cook the liquid until it is reduced to approximately 17.5 cl (6 fl oz) – about 15 minutes. Pour the reduced wine into a bowl and refrigerate it until it is cool – approximately 20 minutes. Stir the crème de cassis into the cooled liquid, then return the sauce to the refrigerator.

With a small, sharp knife, cut a cross in the top of each fig, slicing no more than half way through. Carefully cut each quarter half way down into two or three small wedges, leaving the wedges attached at the bottom; each fig will have eight to twelve wedges in all. With your fingers, press the base of the fig to spread the wedges outwards like the petals of a flower in bloom. (More cutting may be needed to seperate the wedges.)

Set two fig flowers on each of six chilled dessert plates. Dribble some of the sauce over the flowers, then garnish each serving with fresh mint leaves.

Peaches with Mint and Champagne

Serves 4

Working
me: about
) minutes

otal time:
about
hours and
) minutes

Calories
135

Protein
1g

Cholesterol
0mg

Total fat
0g

Saturated fat
0g

Sodium
3mg

	ripe peaches	6	12.5 cl	chilled dry champagne or	4 fl oz
	orange, juice only	1		other sparkling white wine	
	lime, juice only	1	1	fresh mint sprig for garnish	1
osp	honey	2 tbsp		lime slices for garnish	
bsp	chopped fresh mint	4 tbsp			

nch the peaches in boiling water for
seconds, then drain them and run cold water
er them to arrest their cooking. Peel the
aches and halve them lengthwise, discarding
stones.Thinly slice eight of the peach halves
gthwise; transfer the slices to a bowl. Put the
r remaining peach halves into a food processor
a blender along with the orange juice, lime
ce and honey, and purée the mixture. Blend
he chopped mint, then pour the purée over
peach slices. Cover the bowl and chill it for
ours.

With a slotted spoon, transfer the peaches to
a serving platter. Stir the champagne into the
purée remaining in the bowl, and spoon the
purée over the peaches. Garnish the peaches
with the mint sprig and the lime slices just before
serving them.

Editor's Note: There is no need to buy a large
bottle of champagne for this recipe; small bottles
are available.

Grapefruit with Grand Marnier

Serves 6

Working
time: about
30 minutes

Total time:
about
1 hour and
30 minutes
(includes
chilling)

Calories
225

Protein
2g

Cholesterc
0mg

Total fat
0g

Saturated f
0g

Sodium
1mg

2	limes	2	135 g	sugar	4½
2	oranges	2	12.5 cl	Grand Marnier or other	4 fl
2	lemons	2		orange-flavoured liquer	
4	grapefruits	4			

Use a vegetable peeler to pare strips of rind from
the limes, oranges, lemons and grapefruits. Cut
the strips into julienne. Halve the limes, oranges
and lemons, squeeze out the juice and strain it.
Pour the juice into a saucepan. Add the julienned
citrus rind, the sugar, the liqueur and
6 tablespoons of water to the pan; bring the
liquid to the boil. Reduce the heat and simmer

the mixture until it is syrupy – about 10 minut

Peel the grapefruits. Working over a bowl
catch the juice, segment them. Transfer t
segments and their juice to a heatproof bo
Pour the hot syrup over the grapefruit segme
and refrigerate the bowl for 1 hour befc
serving.

Plums with Cream

Serves 6

Working time: about 20 minutes

Total time: about 1 hour and 15 minutes (includes chilling)

Calories 135

Protein 1g

Cholesterol 9mg

Total fat 3g

Saturated fat 2g

Sodium 8mg

| 50 g | ripe purple plums, halved and stoned | 1½ lb | 3 tbsp | arrowroot, mixed with ¼ litre (8 fl oz) water | 3 tbsp |
| tbsp | sugar | 4 tbsp | 6 tbsp | single cream | 6 tbsp |

ombine the plums, sugar and the arrowroot ixture in a large, heavy-bottomed ucepan. Bring the plum mixture to a simmer ver medium heat, stirring constantly. Reduce e heat to maintain a slow simmer and cover e pan. Cook the plums, stirring them from time time, until they become very soft – about) minutes.

Transfer the plums to a food processor or a blender, and purée them. Strain the purée through a sieve into a large bowl. Ladle the purée into six small serving bowls. Cover the bowls and chill them for at least 30 minutes. Spoon 2 tablespoons of the cream over each portion and serve.

Strawberries with Lemon-Strawberry Sauce

Serves 8

Working
(and total)
time: about
45 minutes

Calories
155

Protein
2g

Cholesterol
70mg

Total fat
2g

Saturated fat
0g

Sodium
19mg

2	eggs	2
175 g	caster sugar	6 oz
4 tbsp	cornflour	4 tbsp
2	lemons, grated rind only	2

12.5 cl	fresh lemon juice	4 fl c
1 kg	strawberries, hulled and halved	2 l
1	carambola (star fruit), thinly sliced (optional)	

In a heavy-bottomed saucepan, whisk together the eggs and the sugar; then mix in the cornflour, lemon rind, lemon juice and 12.5 cl (4 fl oz) of water. Set the lemon mixture over medium heat and stir it continuously until it comes to the boil. Continue cooking and stirring the mixture until it is quite thick – about 2 minutes more. Set the mixture aside to cool.

Purée 150 g (5 oz) of the strawberries in food processor or blender. Mix the lemo mixture into the purée. To serve, spoon some c the lemon-strawberry sauce into eight desse glasses or bowls. Carefully set the remainin strawberries in the sauce; garnish each servin if you like, with carambola slices.

Black Forest Cherries

Serves 4

Working
(and total)
time: about
30 minutes

Calories
225

Protein
2g

Cholesterol
20mg

Total fat
7g

Saturated fat
4g

Sodium
75mg

500 g	sweet cherries	1 lb	4 tbsp	double cream	4 tbsp
4 tbsp	sugar	4 tbsp	4 tbsp	kirsch	4 tbsp
1 tbsp	unsweetened cocoa powder	1 tbsp	½ tsp	pure vanilla extract	½ tsp
⅛ tsp	salt	⅛ tsp			

Stone the cherries.

Combine 4 tablespoons of water with the sugar in a heavy saucepan set over medium-high heat, and bring the mixture to the boil. Add the cherries and stir gently to coat them with the syrup. Cook the cherries for 1 minute. Using a slotted spoon, transfer the poached cherries to a gratin dish or other fireproof serving dish, and set the dish aside. Remove the saucepan with the syrup from the heat.

Preheat the grill.

In a bowl, combine the cocoa and salt. Pouring in a steady stream, whisk the cream into the cocoa and salt. Stir the mixture into the syrup in the saucepan. Bring the sauce to the boil, then reduce the heat, and simmer the mixture, stirring occasionally, until it is reduced by half – about 15 minutes. (There should be about 4 tablespoons of thick sauce.) Stir in the kirsch and vanilla extract, then pour the sauce over the cherries. Grill the cherries for 2 to 3 minutes. Serve the cherries for 2 to 3 minutes. Serve the cherries hot, with a spoonful of sauce dribbled over each portion.

Poached Peaches with Berry Sauce

Serves 8

Working time: about 30 minutes

Total time: about 2 hours and 30 minutes (includes chilling)

Calories 120

Protein 1g

Cholesterol 10mg

Total fat 3g

Saturated fat 2g

Sodium 4mg

8	firm but ripe peaches	8
½ litre	dry white wine	16 fl oz
200 g	sugar	7 oz
5 cm	strip of lemon rind	2 inch
8	mint sprigs (optional)	8

	Berry Sauce	
175 g	fresh or frozen blackberries or raspberries	6 oz
2 tbsp	caster sugar	2 tbsp
4 tbsp	double cream	4 tbsp

Blanch the peaches in boiling water until their skins loosen – 30 seconds to 1 minute. Remove the peaches and run cold water over them to arrest the cooking. When the peaches are cool enough to handle, peel them and cut them in half lengthwise, discarding the stones.

Put the wine, sugar and lemon rind into a large saucepan. Bring the liquid to the boil, then reduce the heat, and simmer the mixture for 5 minutes. Add the peach halves to the liquid and poach them until they are just tender – 3 to 5 minutes. Using a slotted spoon, transfer the peach halves to a plate. Discard the poaching syrup. Cover the plate and refrigerate it for at least 2 hours.

To make the berry sauce, purée 125 g (4 oz) of the berries with the caster sugar in a food processor or a blender, then strain the purée through a fine sieve into a jug or bowl and stir in the cream.

To serve, arrange two peach halves on each of eight dessert plates and pour a little of the berry sauce over each portion. Garnish each serving with a few of the remaining berries and, if you like, a sprig of mint.

um-Soused Plantains with Oranges and Kiwi Fruits

Serves 6

Working
and total)
me: about
5 minutes

Calories
200

Protein
1g

Cholesterol
10mg

Total fat
4g

Saturated fat
2g

Sodium
4mg

	oranges	2	6 tbsp	dark rum	6 tbsp
bsp	caster sugar	4 tbsp	2	ripe kiwi fruits	2
g	unsalted butter	1 oz	1 tbsp	icing sugar	1 tbsp
	large ripe plantains, peeled and sliced diagonally into 1 cm (½ inch) pieces	2			

ueeze the juice from one of the oranges.
ain the juice into a small bowl and whisk the
ster sugar into it. Set the bowl aside. Peel the
cond orange; working over another bowl to
ch the juice, segment the second orange. Set
segments aside. Strain the juice in the second
wl into the sweetened juice.

Melt the butter in a large frying pan over
edium-high heat. Add the plantain slices and
ok them for 2 minutes. Turn the plantains over
d cook them on the second side for 2 minutes.
Pour the orange juice over the plantains and
ntinue cooking until the liquid reaches a
mmer. Cook the plantains at a simmer for
minutes. Pour all but 1 tablespoon of the rum
er the plantains. Turn the plantains over and

cook until they are soft – 2 to 4 minutes more.

Remove the pan from the heat; with a slotted
spoon, transfer the plantain slices to a fireproof
baking dish. Reserve the liquid in the pan.
Arrange the plantain slices in the dish, inserting
the orange segments among them.

Peel and chop one of the kiwi fruits, and press
it through a sieve into the liquid in the pan. Stir
the fruit into the liquid, then pour over the
plantain and orange. Peel, quarter, and slice the
other kiwi fruit; set the slices aside.

Sprinkle the icing sugar over the contents of
the baking dish, set the dish below a preheated
grill just long enough to melt the sugar. Garnish
with the kiwi slices. Dribble the remaining
tablespoon of rum over all and serve immediately.

Strawberry Blossoms with Pears and Red Wine Sauce

Serves 8

Working (and total) time: about 45 minutes

Calories 225
Protein 1g
Cholesterol 4mg
Total fat 3g
Saturated fat 1g
Sodium 5mg

60 cl	red wine	1 pint	
135 g	sugar	4½ oz	
1.5 kg	firm, ripe pears, peeled, quartered and cored	3 lb	

15 g	unsalted butter	½	
2 tbsp	fresh lemon juice	2 tb	
750 g	strawberries, hulled	1½	

Combine the wine and half of the sugar in a heavy saucepan over medium heat. Cook the wine, stirring occasionally, until it is reduced to about ¼ litre (8 fl oz) – about 30 minutes. Transfer the sauce to a bowl and refrigerate it until it is cool.

While the wine is reducing, cut the pears into thin strips. Melt the butter in a large, shallow, heavy-bottomed pan over medium heat. Add the pears, lemon juice and the remaining sugar; cook the mixture, stirring frequently, until almost all the liquid has evaporated – 15 to 20 minutes. Transfer the pear mixture to a plate and refrigerate it until it is cool.

Set eight of the smaller berries aside. Stand the remaining strawberies on a cutting board and cut

them into verticle slices about 3 mm (⅛ inc) thick.

Spoon about 4 tablespoons of chilled pe mixture into the centre of a large dessert pla Arrange some of the larger strawberry slices i ring inside the pear mixture, overlapping t slices and propping them at a slight angle resemble the petals of a flower. Form a sma ring of strawberry slices inside the first and sta a whole berry in the centre. Repeat the proce with the remaining pear mixture and strawberr to form eight portions in all.

Just before serving, pour a little of the red wi sauce round the outside of each blossom, letti a few drops fall on to the petals themselves.

Pineapple Gratin

Serves 6

Working time: about 20 minutes

Total time: about 30 minutes

Calories 170

Protein 2g

Cholesterol 45mg

Total fat 1g

Saturated fat 0g

Sodium 20mg

	large ripe pineapple	**1**	½ tsp	pure vanilla extract	**½ tsp**
tbsp	raisins	**2 tbsp**	¼ tsp	ground ginger	**¼ tsp**
tbsp	sultanas	**2 tbsp**	1 tbsp	cornflour	**1 tbsp**
tbsp	pure maple syrup	**5 tbsp**	2	egg whites, at room temperature	**2**
tbsp	bourbon or white rum	**3 tbsp**			
	egg yolk	**1**	2 tbsp	dark brown sugar	**2 tbsp**

Preheat the oven to 240°C (475°F or Mark 9).

Trim and peel the pineapple. Cut it in half from top to bottom. Remove the core from each half by cutting a shallow V-shaped groove down the centre, then cut each half crosswise into nine slices.

Overlap the pineapple slices in a large, shallow baking dish. Scatter the raisins and sultanas over the pineapple slices. Dribble 2 tablespoons of the maple syrup over the top, then sprinkle the dish with 2 tablespoons of the bourbon rum. Cover the dish and set it aside at room temperature.

In a small bowl, blend the egg yolk with the vanilla extract, ginger, cornflour, the remaining maple syrup and the remaining bourbon or rum. In a separate bowl, beat the two egg whites until they form soft peaks. Stir half of the beaten egg whites into the yolk mixture to lighten it. Gently fold the yolk mixture into the remaining beaten egg whites.

Bake the dish containing the pineapple until the slices are heated through – about 3 minutes. Remove the dish from the oven and spread the egg mixture evenly over the fruit. Rub the sugar through a sieve over the top of the egg mixture. Return the dish to the oven and bake the pineapple until the sugar melts and the topping browns and puffs up slightly – about 5 minutes. Serve the gratin immediately.

Mixed Berry Cobbler

Serves 8

Working (and total) time: about 30 minutes

Calories 180

Protein 2g

Cholesterol 10mg

Total fat 6g

Saturated fat 3g

Sodium 5mg

250 g	fresh or frozen raspberries, thawed	8 oz
300 g	fresh or frozen blackberries, thawed	10 oz
300 g	fresh or frozen blueberries, thawed, or other berries	10 oz
4 tbsp	fresh lemon juice	4 tbsp
4 tbsp	sugar	4 tbsp

Oatmeal Topping		
100 g	rolled oats	3½ oz
4 tbsp	dark brown sugar	4 tbsp
45 g	unsalted butter	1½ oz

Preheat the oven to 180°C (350°F or Mark 4).

To prepare the topping, combine the oats and brown sugar in a small bowl. Spread the mixture in a baking tin and bake it until it turns light brown – 8 to 10 minutes. Cut the butter into small pieces and scatter them in the tin. Return the tin to the oven until the butter has melted – about 1 minute. Stir the oats to coat them with the butter and bake the mixture for 5 minutes more. Set the oatmeal topping aside to cool. (The topping may be made ahead and stored, tightly covered, for several days.)

Put half of each of the berries into a large bowl and set them aside. Combine the lemon juice with the sugar in a saucepan and bring the mixture to the boil. Add the remaining blueberries to the syrup; reduce the heat to low and cook the fruit for 3 minutes. Add the remaining raspberries along with the remaining blackberries. Bring the mixture to a simmer and cook it, stirring constantly, for 3 minutes. Pour the cooked fruit into a sieve set over the bowl of reserved berries; use the back of a wooden spoon to press the fruit through the sieve. Stir gently to coat the whole berries with the sauce.

To serve, spoon the warm fruit mixture into individual ramekins or small bowls. Sprinkle some of the topping over each portion.

Nectarine Cobbler

Serves 8

Working time: about 30 minutes

Total time: about 1 hour and 20 minutes

Calories 285

Protein 6g

Cholesterol 40mg

Total fat 4g

Saturated fat 2g

Sodium 175mg

8	large ripe nectarines	**8**
6 tbsp	light brown sugar	**6 tbsp**
½ tsp	ground cinnamon	**½ tsp**
½ tsp	grated nutmeg	**½ tsp**
1 tbsp	fresh lemon juice	**1 tbsp**
2 tbsp	caster sugar	**2 tbsp**

	Cake Topping	
215 g	plain flour	**7½ oz**
1½ tsp	baking powder	**1½ tsp**
¼ tsp	salt	**¼ tsp**
100 g	caster sugar	**3½ oz**
15 g	cold unsalted butter	**½ oz**
1	egg	**1**
17.5 cl	semi-skimmed milk	**6 fl oz**
1 tsp	pure vanilla extract	**1 tsp**

Preheat the oven to 190°C (375°F or Mark 5). Halve the nectarines lengthwise, discarding the stones. Thinly slice the nectarine halves lengthwise. In a bowl, gently toss the slices with the brown sugar, cinnamon, nutmeg and lemon juice. Transfer the contents of the bowl to a large, shallow baking dish and spread out the nectarine slices in an even layer.

For the cake topping, sift the flour, baking powder, salt and caster sugar into a bowl. Cut in the butter with a pastry blender or two knives, blending the mixture just long enough to give it a fine-meal texture. In a separate bowl, mix together the egg, milk and vanilla extract, then pour this mixture into the bowl containing the flour. Using a fork, stir fry the mixture briskly just until it is well blended – about 30 seconds.

Dot the nectarine slices with evenly spaced spoonfuls of the topping, then smooth the topping so that it covers the fruit. Bake the cobbler for 20 minutes, then sprinkle the 2 tablespoons of sugar over the top. Continue baking the cobbler until the topping is brown, puffed and firm, and the juices bubble up around the edges – 20 to 30 minutes more.

Pear and Cranberry Crisp

Serves 8

Working time: about 30 minutes

Total time: about 1 hour and 10 minutes

Calories 190

Protein 3g

Cholesterol 8mg

Total fat 5g

Saturated fat 2g

Sodium 2mg

1	lemon	**1**
200 g	fresh or frozen cranberries	**7 oz**
6 tbsp	sugar	**6 tbsp**
4	pears	**4**

Oat Topping		
140 g	rolled oats	**4½ oz**
4 tbsp	unsweetened apple juice	**4 tbsp**
30 g	unsalted butter, melted	**1 oz**

With a vegetable peeler, pare the rind from the lemon. Chop the rind finely and set it aside. Squeeze the lemon, straining and reserving the juice.

Combine the cranberries with 4 tablespoons of the sugar, the lemon rind and 4 tablespoons of water in a saucepan over medium-high heat. Bring the mixture to the boil and cook it, stirring occasionally, until the berries burst – about 10 minutes. Set aside.

Peel and core the pears, then coarsely chop them. Transfer the pears to a heavy-botttomed saucepan. Dribble the lemon juice over the pears and bring the mixture to the boil. Reduce the heat to maintain a simmer, then cook the mixture, stirring occasionally, until the pears reach the consistency of thick apple sauce – 20 to 30 minutes.Set the pears aside.

Preheat the oven to 200°C (400°F or Mark 6).
For the topping, mix together the oats, apple juice and butter. Spread the oat mixture on a baking sheet and bake it, stirring occasionally, until it has browned – 20 to 30 minutes. Remove the topping from the oven and reduce the temperature to 180°C (350°F or Mark 4).

Spread about 2 tablespoons of the oat mixture in the bottom of a lightly oiled 1.5 litre (2½ pint) baking dish. Spread half of the pear mixture in the dish, then top it with half of the cranberry mixture in an even layer. Spead half of the remaining oat topping over the cranberry mixture. Repeat the layering process with the remaining pear, cranberry and oat mixtures to fill the dish. Sprinkle the remaining 2 tablespoons of sugar on top. Bake the crisp until the juices are bubbling hot in the centre – 20 to 30 minutes.

Apple Brown Betty with Cheddar Cheese

Serves 6

Working time: about 30 minutes

Total time: about 1 hour and 15 minutes

Calories 255

Protein 5g

Cholesterol 11mg

Total fat 4g

Saturated fat 2g

Sodium 170mg

	firm wholemeal bread slices, crusts removed	6	½ tsp	ground cinnamon	½ tsp
	large tart green apples	6	1 tbsp	fresh lemon juice	1 tbsp
125 g	caster sugar	4 oz	12.5 cl	unsweetened apple juice	4 fl oz
			60 g	mature Cheddar cheese, grated	2 oz

Preheat the oven to 150°C (300°F or Mark 2). Cut the bread slices into 1 cm (½ inch) cubes and spread them out on a baking sheet. Bake the bread cubes for 10 minutes, stirring them once to ensure that they cook evenly without browning. Remove the bread cubes from the oven and set them aside. Increase the oven temperature to 190°C (375°F or Mark 5).

Peel, quarter and core the apples, then cut the quarters into thin slices. In a bowl, gently toss the slices with 100 g (3½ oz) of the sugar, the cinnamon, lemon juice and apple juice. Spoon half of the apple mixture into a 1.5 litre (2½ pint) baking dish. Cover the apple mixture with half of the toasted bread cubes. Form another layer with the remaining apple mixture and then the bread cubes. Scatter the grated Cheddar cheese over the bread cubes and sprinkle the remaining sugar evenly on top.

Bake the dish until the juices bubble up around the edges and the top browns – about 45 minutes.

Baked Apples Filled with Grapes

Serves 8		
Working time: about 50minutes		
Total time: about 1 hour and 40 minutes		

Calories 165	
Protein 1g	
Cholesterc 11mg	
Total fat 5g	
Saturated f 3g	
Sodium 5mg	

8	tart apples, cored	**8**
¾ litre	Gewürtztraminer or Riesling	**1¼ pints**
325 g	seedless grapes, picked over	**11 oz**

½ tsp	ground mace	**½ t**
45 g	unsalted butter	**1½**

Preheat the oven to 200°C (400°F or Mark 6).

With a paring knife, cut a ring of semicircles in the skin at the top of each apple; as the apples bake, the semicircles will 'blossom' in a floral pattern. Stand the apples upright in a 5 cm (2 inch) deep baking dish and pour 12.5 cl (4 fl oz) of the wine over them. Put the apples into the oven and bake them for 30 minutes.

While the apples are baking, boil the remaining wine in a saucepan over medium-high heat until only about ¼ litre (8 fl oz) remains. Stir the grapes and mace into the wine, then reduce the heat, and simmer the mixture for 30 seconds.

With a slotted spoon, remove the grapes fro their cooking liquid and set them aside; reserv the liquid.

Spoon the grapes into the apples. Cut th butter into eight pieces and dot each apple wi one piece of the butter. Pour the reduced win over all and return the dish to the oven. Bake th apples until they are tender when pierced wi the tip of a knife – 15 to 30 minutes more.

To serve, transfer the apples to individu plates. If necessary, use a knife to open u the 'flower petals' you carved in the top the apples.

Champagne Jelly with Grapes

Serves 6

Working time: about 20 minutes

Total time: about 4 hours (includes chilling)

Calories 185

Protein 3g

Cholesterol 0mg

Total fat 0g

Saturated fat 0g

Sodium 8mg

750 g	seedless grapes, stemmed and washed	1½ lb	4 tbsp	sugar	4 tbsp
5 tsp	powdered gelatine	5 tsp	¼ litre	chilled dry champagne	16 fl oz

Divide the grapes among six 17.5 cl (6 fl oz) moulds; the grapes should fill each mould no more than three-quarters full. (Alternatively, put all the grapes in a single 1.5 litre/2½ pint mould.) Refrigerate the moulds.

Pour ¼ litre (8 fl oz) of water into the top of a double boiler set over simmering water. Sprinkle in the gelatine and heat the mixture, stirring occasionally, until the gelatine dissolves. Add the sugar and stir until it too dissolves. Remove the gelatine mixture from the heat and pour it into a small bowl.

Set the small bowl in a larger bowl filled with ice. Stir the gelatine mixture until it has cooled to room temperature. Immediately add the champagne, pouring it against the inside of the bowl to preserve as many bubbles as possible.

With a spoon, gently blend the champagne into the gelatine mixture. Ladle the champagne-gelatine mixture into the moulds; spoon the foam that rises to the top back into the bowl. Repeat the ladling process until the moulds are filled to their brims and all the grapes are covered by the liquid. Freeze the moulds for 30 minutes, then chill them for at least 3 hours.

At serving time, dip the bottom of a mould in hot water for 3 seconds; run a knife around the inside of the mould to break the suction, then invert a chilled plate on top, and turn both over together. Lift away the mould. (If the dessert does not unmould, hold the mould firmly on the plate and give them a brisk shake.) Repeat the process to unmould the other desserts and serve them immediately.

Strawberries and Melon in Fruit Jelly

Serves 6

Working time: about 30 minutes

Total time: about 2 hours (includes chilling)

Calories 115

Protein 3g

Cholesterol 0mg

Total fat 1g

Saturated fat 0g

Sodium 12mg

2½ tsp	powdered gelatine	2½ tsp	
12.5 cl	fresh orange juice	4 fl oz	
30 cl	fresh grapefruit juice	½ pint	
4 tbsp	unsweetened white grape juice	4 tbsp	
1 tbsp	fresh lime juice	1 tbsp	
2 tbsp	caster sugar	2 tbsp	
1	melon, halved and seeded	1	

75 g	strawberries	2½ oz
1	kiwi fruit, peeled, thinly sliced crosswise	1
	Strawberry Sauce	
150 g	strawberries	5 oz
1 tbsp	caster sugar	1 tbsp
½ tbsp	fresh lime juice	½ tbsp

Put 3 tablespoons of water into a small bowl; sprinkle in the gelatine and let it stand until it has absorbed all the water and is transparent – about 5 minutes. Combine the fruit juices and the sugar in a pan; bring to the boil, then immediately remove from the heat. Add the gelatine mixture and stir until the gelatine is dissolved. Chill the fruit-jelly liquid until it is syrupy – about 30 minutes – then keep it at room temperature.

With a melon baller, scoop out the melon flesh. Put 3 or 4 melon balls in a single layer into each of six ramekins. Pour enough of the fruit jelly mixture into each to barely cover the melon. Chill until the jelly sets. Slice the 75 g

(2½ oz) of strawberries in half lengthwise. Arrange, cut sides facing out and stem ends up, round the edge of each ramekin. Fill the ramekins with melon and cover the fruit with the remaining mixture. Chill until jelly sets – at least 1 hour.

To make the strawberry sauce, purée the sauce ingredients in a processor/blender. Cover and chill.

When the jelly is set, run the tip of a knife round the inside edge of each ramekin. Invert a chilled plate over a ramekin, turn them both over and lift away the ramekin. Pour some of the strawberry sauce round each portion; garnish with the kiwi slices and remaining melon balls.

Glazed Fruit Tartlets

**Makes
16 tartlets**

**Working
time: about
1 hour**

**Total time:
about
1 hour and
30 minutes**

Per tartlet:

Calories
120

Protein
3g

Cholesterol
5mg

Total fat
4g

Saturated fat
2g

Sodium
110mg

40 g	sifted plain flour	5 oz	300 g	redcurrant jelly or apricot jam	10 oz
0 g	cold unsalted butter	1 oz	125 g	fresh raspberries	4 oz
5 g	polyunsaturated margarine	½ oz			
tsp	salt	¼ tsp		**Cream Filling**	
tbsp	caster sugar	2 tbsp	175 g	low-fat cottage cheese	6 oz
tsp	pure vanilla extract	¼ tsp	1	lemon, grated rind only	1
	ripe nectarines	2	2 tbsp	caster sugar	2 tbsp

Preheat the oven to 200°C (400°F or Mark 6).

To prepare the dough, put the flour, butter, margarine, salt and sugar into a processor and blend to a fine-meal texture. Add the vanilla and 2 tablespoons of water, and blend until the mixture forms a ball. Shape into a log about 20 cm (8 inches) long, then wrap in plastic film, and chill. For the filling, purée the cottage cheese in the food processor so that the curd is no longer visible, then blend in the lemon rind and the sugar. Refrigerate.

To form the shells, divide the dough into 16 equal pieces. Press each piece into a fluted 10 by 5 cm (4 by 2 inch) boat-shaped tartlet tin or a fluted 6 cm (2½ inch) round tartlet tin. Freeze the shells for 10 minutes. Set the shells on a baking sheet and bake until their edges start to brown – 6 to 8 minutes. Leave the shells in their tins to cool.

Halve the nectarines lengthwise, discarding the stones, thinly slice the halves. Melt the jelly or sieved jam in a small pan over medium heat, stirring to prevent sticking. Allow to cool until thick enough to coat the fruit.

To assemble the desserts, spread about 2 teaspoons of the chilled filling inside each tartlet shell. Arrange the fruit on the filling. Brush the fruit lightly with the warm jelly. If the jelly cools to room temperature, reheat it, stirring, until it is thin enough to spread.

Gingery Peach and Almond Tartlets

Serves 10

Working
time: about
45 minutes

Total time:
about
1 hour and
30 minutes

Calories
150

Protein
3g

Cholesterol
60mg

Total fat
6g

Saturated fat
1g

Sodium
35mg

5	firm but ripe peaches	5
75 g	blanched almonds	2½ oz
4 tbsp	plain flour	4 tbsp
½ tsp	baking powder	½ tsp

½ tbsp	finely chopped fresh ginger root	½ tbsp
100 g	caster sugar	3½ oz
2	eggs	2
15 g	unsalted butter, softened	½ oz

Blanch the peaches in boiling water until their skins loosen – 30 seconds to 1 minute. Peel the peaches, then cut them in half, discarding the stones.

Preheat the oven to 170°C (325°F or Mark 3).

Put the almonds, flour, baking powder, ginger and sugar into a food processor or a blender; blend the mixture until the nuts are finely chopped. Add the eggs and butter, and process them just long enough to blend them in.

Slice one of the peach halves lengthwise and

arrange the slices in a lightly oiled 10 cm (4 inch) tartlet tin. Cut and arrange the remaining peach halves the same way. Spoon the almond mixture over the peaches and bake the tartlets until they are lightly browned – 30 to 40 minutes.

Let the tartlets cool on a wire rack, then remove them from the tins and serve.

Editor's Note: These tartlets may be made in a muffin tin.

Cornmeal Tartlets with Tapioca-Blueberry Filling

Serves 8

Working time: about 20 minutes

Total time: about 1 hour and 30 minutes

Calories 273

Protein 3g

Cholesterol 7mg

Total fat 6g

Saturated fat 2g

Sodium 170mg

175 g	plain flour	6 oz		**Tapioca-Blueberry Filling**	
0 g	cornmeal	2 oz	600 g	fresh blueberries, picked	1¼ lb
0 g	icing sugar	2 oz		over and stemmed, or frozen	
tsp	salt	½ tsp		blueberries, thawed	
tbsp	cornflour	1 tbsp	100 g	caster sugar	3½ oz
0 g	cold unsalted butter, cut into	1 oz	1 tbsp	fresh lemon juice	1 tbsp
	4 pieces		2 tsp	grated lemon rind	2 tsp
0 g	cold polyunsaturated margarine,	1 oz	1 tbsp	tapioca	1 tbsp
	cut into 4 pieces				

o prepare the tartlet dough, combine the flour, ornmeal, icing sugar, salt and cornflour in a rocessor or a bowl. If using a processor, add the ts, and cut them into the ingredients with short ursts. With the motor running, pour in 2 tbsp of old water in a thin stream, blending the dough nto a ball. If the dough is too crumbly, add up o 1 tbsp of water. If making the dough in a bowl ut the fats into the ingredients, then mix in the rater. Wrap in plastic film and refrigerate for 0 minutes.

Scatter several tbsps of cornmeal over a work urface and roll the dough to 3 mm (⅛ inch) nick. Cut the dough in rounds about 11 cm

(4½ inches) in diameter and use to line eight 7.5 cm (3 inch) tartlet moulds. Chill in the freezer for at least 10 minutes. Heat the oven to 200°C (400°F or Mark 6).

Bake the shells until browned and crisp – 20 to 25 minutes. Remove from moulds and cool.

To prepare the filling, mix the blueberries, sugar, lemon juice and rind in a pan. Bring to the boil over medium heat, cook until the berries burst and there is about ¼ litre (8 fl oz) of juice in the pan. Add tapioca and cook stirring, until it thickens slightly. Allow to cool, then spoon into the shells and stand for 10 minutes before serving.

Apple Sorbet with Candied almonds

Serves 8

Working time: about 50 minutes

Total time: about 1 to 3 hours, depending on freezing method

Calories 250

Protein 1g

Cholesterol 0mg

Total fat 2g

Saturated fat 0g

Sodium 2mg

10	tart green apples	**10**
5	lemons, juice only	**5**
330 g	caster sugar	**11 oz**

30 g	slivered almonds	**1**
1 tbsp	brown sugar	**1 tbs**

Cut off and discard the top quarter of one of the apples. Using a melon baller or spoon, scoop the flesh, core and seeds from the apple, leaving a 5 mm (¼ inch) thick wall. Reserve the flesh; discard the core and seeds. Sprinkle the inside of the apple and the reserved flesh with some of the lemon juice. Repeat the process with all but two of the remaining apples, then freeze the hollowed apples. Peel, seed and chop the two remaining apples, and add them to the reserved flesh.

Put ½ litre (16 fl oz) of water, 200 g (7 oz) of the sugar and about half of the remaining lemon juice in a saucepan. Bring the liquid to the boil, reduce the heat to medium, and simmer for 3 minutes. Add the reserved apple flesh and simmer it until it is tender – 3 to 4 minutes. With a slotted spoon, transfer the cooked apple to a food processor or blender. Discard the poaching

liquid. Purée the apple; put ½ litre (16 fl oz) of the purée into a bowl and allow it to cool. If an purée is left over, reserve it for another use.

Stir the remaining lemon juice and th remaining sugar into the apple purée. Freez the mixture.

While the sorbet is freezing, put the slivere almonds in a small, heavy frying pan ove medium heat. Toast the almonds, stirrin constantly, until they turn golden-brown – abou 5 minutes. Stir in the brown sugar, increase th heat to high, and cook the almonds until the are coated with melted sugar – about 1 minut more. Set the almonds aside.

When the sorbet is firm, scoop or spoon it in the prepared apple cups, then sprinkle some o the candied almonds over each apple. Keep th apples in the freezer until they are served.

Plum and Red Wine Sorbet with Raisin Sauce

Serves 10

Working
time: about
25 minutes

Total time:
about 1 day

Calories
180

Protein
1g

Cholesterol
0mg

Total fat
0g

Saturated fat
0g

Sodium
3mg

60 cl	red wine	1 pint	2 tbsp	fresh lemon juice	2 tbsp
250 g	sugar	8 oz	45 g	raisins	1½ oz
500 g	ripe red plums, quartered and stoned, two of the quarters sliced for garnish	1 lb	45 g	sultanas	1½ oz

Combine ½ litre (16 fl oz) of the wine with the sugar in a saucepan over medium heat. Bring to the boil, stirring to dissolve the sugar. Reduce the heat, cover the pan, and simmer for 2 minutes. Stir in the plum quarters; as soon as the syrup returns to a simmer, cover the pan again and cook the plums for 4 minutes more. Strain 12.5 cl (4 fl oz) of the syrup into a small bowl and set it aside for the sauce.

Purée the plum-wine mixture in a blender/ processor. Blend in the remaining wine and the lemon juice. Let the mixture cool to room temperature, then chill it.

Freeze the sorbet mixture until it is firm but not hard. Transfer the frozen sorbet to a metal mould or bowl. Rap the bottom of the mould or bowl on the counter once or twice to collapse any large air bubbles. Cover the container with plastic film and freeze the sorbet overnight.

To prepare the sauce, combine the reserved 12.5 cl (4 fl oz) of syrup with the raisins and sultanas in a small, heavy-bottomed saucepan. Quickly bring the mixture to the boil, then immediately remove the pan from the heat. Let the sauce cool to room temperature before refrigerating it; the dried fruit will plump up.

Shortly before serving, unmould the sorbet. Dip the bottom of the mould in hot water for 15 seconds; invert a chilled platter on top and turn both over. If it does not unmould, wrap it in a towel which has been soaked in hot water. After 15 seconds, remove the towel and lift the mould away. Garnish the sorbet with the reserved plum slices, then cut the sorbet into wedges. Serve some of the raisin sauce with each portion.

Strawberry and Champagne Sorbet

Serves 6	
Working time: about 15 minutes	
Total time: about 1 to 2 hours depending on freezing method	

Calories	170
Protein	0g
Cholesterol	0mg
Total fat	0g
Saturated fat	0g
Sodium	4mg

350 g	hulled strawberries, quartered and chilled	**12 oz**
150 g	caster sugar	**5 oz**
2 tbsp	fresh lemon juice	**2 tbsp**
½ litre	chilled dry champagne	**16 fl oz**
6	strawberries for garnish	**6**

Put the strawberry quarters, sugar and lemon juice in a food processor or blender; process the mixture briefly so that the berries are finely chopped – not puréed. Add the champagne, pouring it slowly against the inside of the bowl to keep it from frothing. Blend quickly to retain as much effervescence as possible, then freeze the mixture.

Scoop the sorbet into dessert glasses. If you like, garnish each portion with a strawberry and serve with a glass of chilled champagne.

Editor's Note: The success of this recipe depends partly upon starting out with chilled strawberries and champagne.

Frozen Raspberry Yogurt

Serves 6

Working time: about 15 minutes

Total time: about to 3 hours depending on freezing method

Calories	140	
Protein	5g	
Cholesterol	5mg	
Total fat	1g	
Saturated fat	1g	
Sodium	70mg	

)0 g	fresh or frozen raspberries, thawed	10 oz
litre	plain low-fat yogurt	16 fl oz
100 g	caster sugar	3½ oz
2	egg whites	2
4 tbsp	crème de cassis (optional)	4 tbsp

urée the raspberries in a food processor or ender. Then, to remove the raspberry seeds, ass the purée through a fine sieve into a bowl; se a spatula to force the purée through a wire esh. Combine the purée with the yogurt and igar, whisk in the egg whites, then freeze the ixture.

Pass the crème de cassis seperately so that ach diner can pour a little over the yogurt.

Editor's Note: If desired, two yogurts can be swirled together. Make frozen vanilla yogurt. Spoon the frozen raspberry yogurt inside a piping bag, keeping it to one side; spoon the frozen vanilla yogurt on top of the raspberry yogurt, filling the other side of the bag. Pipe out the two yogurts together in a mounting spiral.

Frozen Banana Yogurt with Streusel Crumbs

Serves 8

Working
time: about
15 minutes

Total time:
about
1 to 3 hours,
depending
on freezing
method

Protein
6g

Cholesterol
8mg

Total fat
3g

Saturated fat
2g

Sodium
100mg

350 g	ripe bananas	12 oz
2 tbsp	fresh lemon juice	2 tbsp
¼ litre	plain low-fat yogurt	16 fl oz
2	egg whites, at room temperature	2

6 tbsp	caster sugar	6 tbs
3	slices wholemeal bread	
15 g	unsalted butter	½ o
4 tbsp	light brown sugar	4 tbs
1 tbsp	finely chopped walnuts	1 tbs

Purée the bananas and lemon juice in a food processor or blender. Add the yogurt, egg whites and caster sugar, and blend the mixture for 5 seconds.

Freeze the yogurt mixture.

While the yogurt mixture is freezing, make the streusel: preheat the oven to 170°C (325°F or Mark 3). Tear each slice of bread into three or four pieces; Put the bread pieces in a food processor or a blender and process them until they are reduced to fine crumbs. Spread the crumbs in a baking tin and bake them, stirring once or twice to ensure even cooking, until they

are crisp – about 15 minutes. Cut the butter int small bits and scatter them over the breadcrumb Return the pan to the oven just long enough t melt the butter – about 1 minute. Stir th breadcrumbs to coat them with the butter, the transfer the mixture to a bowl. Stir in the brow sugar and walnuts, and set the mixture aside

When the yogurt mixture is nearly frozen – will still be soft – stir in all but 2 tablespoons o the streusel mixture. Return the yogurt to th freezer for approximately 15 minutes more t firm it up. Just before serving the yogurt, sprinkl the reserved streusel over the top.

Two-Melon Ice with Poppy Seeds and Port Sauce

Serves 8

Working time: about 15 minutes

Total time: about 1 to 3 hours, depending on freezing method

Port Sauce:

Calories 183

Protein 2g

Cholesterol 0mg

Total fat 1g

Saturated fat 0g

Sodium 20mg

	ripe honeydew melon (about 2.5 kg/5 lb)	1	**200 to**		caster sugar, depending on	**7 to**
	ripe cantaloupe melon (about 1.5 kg/3 lb)	1	**275 g**		the sweetness of the melon	**9 oz**
tsp	poppy seeds	1 tsp			**Port Sauce (optional)**	
tsp	ground mace	⅛ tsp	**35 cl**		ruby port	**12 fl oz**
tbsp	fresh lemon juice	4 tbsp	**2 tsp**		cornflour	**2 tsp**

Halve the honeydew melon crosswise, using a zigzag cut. Discard the seeds. Select the more attractive half of the melon for serving; with a melon baller, scoop out balls of flesh. Refrigerate the balls in a bowl. Cut some flesh from the other half and purée it in a processor/blender – about ½ litre (16 fl oz) of purée. If it measures less than ½ litre (16 fl oz), process more melon flesh. Refrigerate the purée.

Slice the cantaloupe in ½ with a crosswise cut. Scoop out one ½ into balls and refrigerate with the honeydew balls until serving time. Cut the remaining cantaloupe ½ into chunks and purée to produce ½ litre (16 fl oz). Stir the cantaloupe and honeydew purées together and chill them.

Using the honeydew half selected for serving, scrape the inside of the shell clean. Pare a thin slice from the bottom so that the melon will stand upright, then freeze the shell.

Combine the melon purée with the poppy seeds, mace, lemon juice and sugar; freeze.

To make the sauce, bring 30 cl (2 pint) of the port to the boil in a saucepan. Combine the remaining port with the cornflour and stir the mixture into the boiling port. Cook, stirring, until it thickens – about 1 minute, then cool and chill.

Fill the frozen honeydew shell with ice-cream scoops of the melon ice. Scatter the chilled melon balls over the top and pass the sauce separately.

Frozen Piña Coladas

Serves 8

Working
time: about
20 minutes

Total time:
about
2 hours and
20 minutes

Calories
125

Protein
3g

Cholesterol
2mg

Total fat
2g

Saturated fat
1g

Sodium
80mg

75 g	fresh pineapple flesh, chopped	**2½ oz**	**2**	egg whites	
75 g	peeled banana, chopped	**2½ oz**	**4 tbsp**	dark rum	**4 tbsp**
¼ litre	buttermilk	**16 fl oz**	**3 tbsp**	shredded coconut for garnish	**3 tbsp**
100 g	caster sugar	**3½ oz**			

Process the pineapple and the banana in a blender or a food processor, stopping once to scrape down the sides with a rubber spatula, until every trace of fibre has disappeared and a smooth purée results – about 1 minute. (There should be approximately ¼ litre/8 fl oz of purée.) Blend in the buttermilk, sugar, egg whites and rum. Freeze the mixture.

Scoop the sorbet into glasses and keep in the freezer until serving time.

To toast the coconut, spread it in a baking tin and set it in a preheated 180°C (350°F or Mark 4) oven. Toast the coconut, stirring every 5 minutes until it is lightly browned – 15 to 20 minutes.

Just before serving the desserts, sprinkle some of the toasted coconut over each one.

Sliced Watermelon Sorbet

Serves 16

Working [ti]me: about [1]0 minutes

[T]otal time: about [1] to 6 hours (includes chilling)

Calories
90

Protein
1g

Cholesterol
0mg

Total fat
1g

Saturated fat
0g

Sodium
3mg

	watermelon (about 3.5 kg/8 lb)	**1**	**2¼ tbsp** fresh lemon juice	**2¼ tbsp**
[20]0 g	caster sugar	**7 oz**	**145 g** fresh blueberries	**5 oz**

[Ha]lve the watemelon lengthwise. Scoop out all [th]e flesh and put into a large bowl. select the [m]ore attractive half of the watermelon to use for [se]rving; discard the other half. Cut the [w]atermelon half crosswise into slices about [2.]5 cm (1 inch) thick. Reassemble the slices so [th]at the watermelon shell appears intact, and [fr]eze it until it is rock-hard and the slices are [fir]mly stuck together. (In order for the slices to [ad]here, it may be necessary to prop the shell in [pl]ace during freezing.)

[Pu]rée the watermelon flesh in several batches [in] a blender or food processor, then press it [thr]ough a sieve to filter out the seeds. Measure [th]e strained fruit; there should be about 1.75 litres

(3 pints). (If you have more or less fruit, increase or decrease the amount of sugar accordingly by 2 tablespoons per ¼ litre/8 fl oz of fruit.) Stir the sugar and lemon juice into the strained fruit, then freeze the mixture. Do not stir the blueberries into the watermelon sorbet until the end of its freezing period.

When the melon shell is frozen solid, fill it with the blueberry-studded sorbet, smoothing the top so that the final result will resemble a freshly cut watermelon half. Freeze the assembly until it is solid throughout – at least 2 hours.

Present the watermelon intact. Using the precut lines as a guide, cut the watermelon into slices.

Spiced Coffee Ice Cream

Serves 8

Working time: about 15 minutes

Total time: 1 to 3 hours, depending on freezing method

Calories
160

Protein
6g

Cholestero
15mg

Total fat
5g

Saturated fa
3g

Sodium
70mg

325 g	low-fat ricotta cheese	**11 oz**
12.5 cl	plain low-fat yogurt	**4 fl oz**
135 g	caster sugar	**4½ oz**
¼ litre	freshly brewed triple-strength coffee, strained and chilled	**8 fl oz**

½ tsp	ground cinnamon	**½ ts**
½ tsp	ground cardamom, or ¼ tsp grated nutmeg	**½ ts**
½ tsp	pure vanilla extract	**½ ts**
30 g	plain chocolate, grated	**1 ¢**

Purée the ricotta, yogurt and sugar in a food processor or blender, stopping at least once to scrape down the sides, until you have a very smooth purée. Whisk the coffee, cinnamon, cardamom or nutmeg, vanilla and chocola into the purée. Freeze. If using the food process method, add the chocolate after processing t mixture.

Frozen Nectarine and Plum Terrine

Serves 10

Working time: about 45 minutes

Total time: about 1 day (includes freezing)

Calories
190

Protein
1g

Cholesterol
0mg

Total fat
1g

Saturated fat
0g

Sodium
1mg

	Nectarine Sorbet	
500 g	nectarines, halved and stoned	**1 lb**
12.5 cl	fresh orange juice	**4 fl oz**
4 tbsp	fresh lemon juice	**4tbsp**
150 g	caster sugar	**5 oz**
	Plum Sorbet	
500 g	plums, halved and stoned	**1 lb**

17.5 cl	fresh orange juice	**6 fl oz**
150 g	caster sugar	**5 oz**
	Garnish	
1	nectarine, halved, stoned and sliced into thin wedges	**1**
2	plums, halved, stoned and sliced into thin wedges	**2**

To prepare the nectarine sorbet, purée the nectarines, orange juice, lemon juice and sugar in a food processor or blender. Transfer the purée to a freezer container and freeze it. Prepare the plum sorbet in the same way and freeze it as well.

When both sorbets are firm but not hard, line a 1.5 litre (2½ pint) loaf tin or metal mould with plastic film.

Put half the nectarine sorbet into the lined tin, smoothing it out with a rubber spatula. Top the nectarine sorbet with half of the plum sorbet;

smooth its top the same way. Repeat the layering process with the remaining sorbet to make four layers in all. To collapse any air bubbles, tap the bottom of the tin on the work surface. Cover the top of the sorbet with plastic film and freeze the terrine overnight.

Remove the plastic film from the top. Invert the terrine on to a chilled platter. Unwrap the terrine and cut it into 1 cm (½ inch) slices, dipping the knife into hot water and wiping it off between slices. Garnish the slices with the wedges of nectarine and plum.

Grape Lollies

Makes 12

Working
time: about
30 minutes

Total time:
about
1 hour and
20 minutes

Calories
70
Protein
0g
Cholesterol
0mg
Total fat
0g
Saturated fat
0g
Sodium
2mg

| **500 g** | seedless green grapes | **1 lb** | **5 tbsp** | caster sugar | **5 tbsp** |
| **500 g** | seedless black grapes | **1 lb** | | | |

Purée the green grapes in a food processor or a blender. Strain the purée through a fine sieve into a small saucepan. Bring the purée to a simmer over medium-high heat, then stir in 2½ tablespoons of the sugar, and remove the pan from the heat. When the mixture has cooled to room temperature, pour it into a 12-space madeleine tray, filling each space to the brim. Reserve the excess purée. Chill the tray in the freezer until the purée has nearly set – about 30 minutes.

Lay the end of a flat ice lolly stick in the centre of each of the six frozen sorbets in the bottom row of the tray; the sticks should overhang the tray's bottom edge. Return the tray to the freezer.

While the tray is chilling, purée the black grapes in a food processor or blender and strain the purée into a saucepan. Bring the purée to a simmer over medium-high heat, then stir in the remaining 2½ tablespoons of sugar, and remove the pan from the heat. Pour the mixture into a bowl and set it aside to cool.

When the green-grape mixture has frozen solid, remove the madeleine tray from the freezer; pop out the sorbets in the top row and brush their flat sides with the reserved green-grape mixture. Set one of the painted sorbets on top a sorbet that is still in the tray, and press it in place. Repeat the process to form six lollies in all, then return the tray to the freezer for 30 minutes.

When the green-grape lollies have frozen solid, remove them from the tray mould and return them to the freezer. Clean the mould and use it to make six black-grape lollies, using the same method.

Editor's note: These frozen confections are formed in a madeleine tray.

Mango Ice Cream

Serves 8

Working time: about 40 minutes

Total time: 1 to 3 hours, depending on freezing method

Calories 155

Protein 3g

Cholesterol 18mg

Total fat 5g

Saturated fat 3g

Sodium 35mg

1.5 kg	ripe mangoes, peeled and stoned	**3 lb**
35 cl	semi-skimmed milk	**12 fl oz**

6 tbsp	double cream	**6 tbsp**
3 tbsp	caster sugar	**3 tbsp**
1	lime, juice only	**1**

Cut enough of the mangoes into small cubes to weigh 250 g (8 oz); chill the cubes in the refrigerator.

Purée the remaining mangoes in a blender or a food processor and transfer the purée to a bowl. (There should be about ½ litre/16 fl oz of purée.) Add the milk, cream, sugar and lime juice, and stir until the sugar dissolves. Freeze the ice cream.

Scoop the ice cream into serving dishes, then serve each portion with some of the chilled mango cubes.

Peach Ice Cream

Serves 8

Working time: about 30 minutes

Total time: 1 to 3 hours, depending on freezing method

Calories 195
Protein 8g
Cholesterol 18mg
Total fat 5g
Saturated fat 3g
Sodium 95mg

1 kg	ripe peaches	**2 lb**	**12.5 cl**	semi-skimmed milk	**4 fl oz**
1½ tbsp	fresh lemon juice	**1½ tbsp**	**75 g**	light brown sugar	**2½ oz**
350 g	low-fat ricotta cheese	**12 oz**	**2**	egg whites	**2**
12.5 cl	plain low-fat yogurt	**4 fl oz**	**½ tsp**	pure vanilla extract	**½ tsp**
2 tbsp	soured cream	**2 tbsp**	**¼ tsp**	almond extract	**¼ tsp**

Bring 2 litres (3½ pints) of water to the boil in a large saucepan. Add the peaches and blanch them until their skins loosen – 30 seconds to 1 minute. Remove the peaches with a slotted spoon and set them aside; when they are cool enough to handle, peel them, cut them in half and remove their stones.

Cut enough of the peach halves into 1 cm (½ inch) dice to weigh about 375 g (13 oz). Purée the remaining peach halves with the lemon juice in a food processor or a blender.

Transfer the peach purée to a large bowl and set it aside.

Put the ricotta, yogurt and soured cream in the food processor or blender; purée the mixture until it has a creamy consistency, stopping at least once to scrape down the sides . Blend in the milk, brown sugar, egg whites, and the vanilla and almond extracts, then whisk the mixture into the peach purée.

Stir the reserved peach dice into the purée and freeze it.

Ginger-Date Ice Cream

Serves 8

Working
me: about
5 minutes

otal time:
to 3 hours,
depending
n freezing
method

Calories
120

Protein
6g

Cholesterol
12mg

Total fat
3g

Saturated fat
2g

Sodium
75mg

itre	semi-skimmed milk	8 fl oz	2 tbsp	caster sugar	2 tbsp
5 g	dried stoned dates, cut into small pieces	4 oz	2	egg whites	2
bsp	plain low-fat yogurt	6 tbsp	1 tbsp	finely chopped crystallized ginger	1 tbsp
0 g	low-fat ricotta cheese	8 oz	½ tbsp	fresh lemon juice	½ tbsp

arm the milk in a saucepan over very low heat.
move the pan from the heat and add all but
ablespoons of the dates; steep the dates for
minutes.
Purée the date-milk mixture in a food processor
a blender, then transfer to a large bowl.
Purée the yogurt, ricotta cheese and sugar in
e food processor or blender, stopping at least
ce to scrape down the sides, until you have a
ry smooth purée. Add the yogurt-ricotta purée
the date-milk purée in the bowl, and whisk the
o together. Refrigerate the bowl for 15 minutes.

Blend the egg whites into the refrigerated
purée, then freeze the mixture. If you plan to use
an ice cream maker, stir the crystallized ginger,
lemon juice and reserved 2 tablespoons of dates
into the mixture before freezing it. If you are
using the hand-whisking method, stir in the
lemon juice, ginger and reserved dates when the
mixture is almost solid. For the food processor
method, add the lemon juice during the
processing, then blend in the ginger and reserved
dates.

Amaretti

Makes about 100 biscuits

Working time: about 30 minutes

Total time: about 9 hours (includes standing time)

Per biscuit

Calories
20

Protein
0g

Cholesterol
0mg

Total fat
1g

Saturated fat
0g

Sodium
9mg

250 g	almond paste	8 oz	4	egg whites	
2 tsp	pure almond extract	2 tsp	⅛ tsp	salt	⅛ t
200 g	caster sugar	7 oz		icing sugar	

Mix together the almond paste, almond extract and 135 g (4½ oz) of the sugar in a bowl. Beating continuously, gradually add about half of the egg whites. Continue beating until the mixture has lightened in texture and colour – about 3 minutes.

To prepare the meringue, beat the remaining egg whites in a bowl until they are foamy. Add the salt, then continue beating the whites until they form soft peaks. Gradually add the remaining sugar, beating all the while, until the whites form stiff peaks.

Fold one third of the meringue into the almond mixture to lighten it, then fold in the remaining meringue. Spoon the mixture into a piping bag fitted with a plain nozzle. Line two baking sheets with non-stick parchment paper and pipe out the mixture in mounds about 2.5 cm (1 inch) across.

Sprinkle the mounds generously with icing sugar and let them stand at room temperature for least 8 hours.

Preheat the oven to 180°C (350°F or Mark 4).

To allow the amaretti to puff during baking, pinch a mound at its base, cracking the surface. Pinch the mound once more to crack its surface a second time at a right angle to the first. Repeat the process to crack all the amaretti.

Bake the amaretti, with the oven door propped slightly ajar with the handle of a wooden spoon, for 30 minutes. Remove the biscuits from the oven and let them stand, still on the paper, until they have cooled to room temperature. Remove the amaretti from the parchment paper, and store them in an airtight container until serving time.

Tuile Brandy Snaps

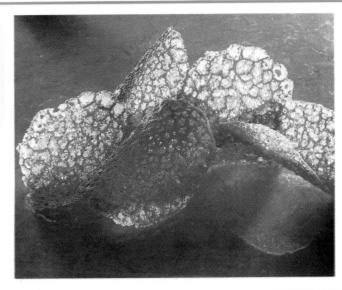

**Makes
12 biscuits**

**Working
time: about
10 minutes**

**Total time:
about
20 minutes**

Per biscuit:

**Calories
54**

**Protein
0g**

**Cholesterol
5mg**

**Total fat
2g**

**Saturated fat
1g**

**Sodium
3mg**

30 g	unsalted butter	1 oz	1 tsp	ground ginger	1 tsp
2 tbsp	sugar	2 tbsp	½ tsp	grated lemon rind	½ tsp
2 tbsp	golden syrup	2 tbsp	2 tbsp	brandy	2 tbsp
1 tsp	molasses	1 tsp	45 g	plain flour	1½ oz

Preheat the oven to 200°C (400°F or Mark 6).

Put the butter, sugar, syrup, molasses, ginger, rind and brandy into a small saucepan and bring the mixture to the boil. Cook the mixture for 1 minute, then remove it from the heat and let it cool for 1 minute. Add the flour and whisk the batter until it is smooth.

Lightly oil a heavy baking sheet. Drop the batter on to the sheet in heaped teaspoonfuls at least 7.5 cm (3 inches) apart. (It may be necessary to bake the biscuits in two batches; if you are using two baking sheets, stagger the cooking to allow enough time to shape the biscuits after

they are baked.) Bake the biscuits until they turn slightly darker – 3 to 4 minutes.

Remove the baking sheet from the oven and let it sit for 1 minute while the biscuits firm up a little. With a metal spatula, remove some of the still-soft biscuits and drape them over a clean rolling pin to cool. Remove the curved biscuits from the rolling pin as soon as they harden – about 30 seconds. Immediately repeat the procedure to fashion the remaining biscuits. If any of the biscuits become hard while they are still on the baking sheet, return them to the oven for a few seconds to soften them.

Baked Chocolate Custards

Serves 8

Working time: about 30 minutes

Total time: about 2 hours

Calories 110
Protein 4g
Cholesterol 75mg
Total fat 3g
Saturated fat 1g
Sodium 70mg

2	eggs	**2**
100 g	caster sugar	**3½ oz**
2 tbsp	unsweetened cocoa powder	**2 tbsp**

	one-sixteenth teaspoon salt	
½ litre	semi-skimmed milk	**16 fl oz**
45 g	fresh raspberries (optional)	**1½ oz**

Preheat the oven to 170°C (325°F or Mark 3). Whisk together the eggs, sugar, cocoa powder and salt in a heatproof bowl. Heat the milk in a small saucepan just until it comes to the boil. Whisking continuously, pour the hot milk into the bowl. Thoroughly mix in the milk, then pour the mixture into the saucepan.

Cook the mixture over low heat, stirring constantly with a wooden spoon, until it has thickened enough to lightly coat the back of the spoon. Strain the mixture into eight individual ovenproof custard cups or ramekins. Set the custard cups in a roasting pan or casserole with sides at least 1 cm (½ inch) higher than the cups. Pour enough boiling water into the pan to come half way up the sides of the cups. Cover the pan with a baking sheet or a piece of aluminium foil, then put it in the oven, and bake the custards until the centre of one barely quivers when the cup is shaken – 20 to 30 minutes.

Remove the pan from the oven and uncover it. Leave the custard cups in the water until they cool to room temperature, then refrigerate them for at least 30 minutes. If you like, arrange several fresh raspberries on each custard before serving them.

Amaretto Custards with Plum Sauce

Serves 6

Working time: about 30 minutes

Total time: about 1 hour and 30 minutes

Calories 250
Protein 8g
Cholesterol 100mg
Total fat 7g
Saturated fat 2g
Sodium 95mg

25 g	almonds, sliced	**¾ oz**	**90 g**	honey	**3 oz**
1¼ tsp	ground cinnamon	**1¼ tsp**	**55 cl**	semi-skimmed milk	**18 fl oz**
5 tbsp	caster sugar	**5 tbsp**	**4**	ripe red plums, quartered	**4**
2	eggs, plus 2 egg whites	**2**		and stoned	
4 tbsp	amaretto liquer	**4 tbsp**	**2 tsp**	fresh lemon juice	**2 tsp**

Preheat the oven to 170°C (325°F or Mark 3). Spread the almonds in a baking tin and toast in the preheating oven until golden – 25 minutes.

Lightly butter six 12.5 cl (4 cl oz) ramekins. In a dish, mix ¾ teaspoon of the cinnamon with 2 tablespoons of the sugar. Put about 1 teaspoon of the mixture into each ramekin, then tilt it in all directions to coat it all over. Put the ramekins into a large baking dish and refrigerate them.

Whisk the eggs, egg whites, amaretto, honey and remaining ½ teaspoon of cinnamon. Whisk in the milk, pour into the chilled ramekins, filling each to within 5 mm (¼ inch) of the top.

Place the baking dish with the ramekins in the preheated oven. Pour enough hot tap water into the baking dish to come ⅝ of the way up the sides of the ramekins. Bake the custards until a

knife inserted in the centre of one comes out clean – about 30 minutes. Remove them from the water and leave standing for ½ an hour.

While the custards cool, combine the plums, the remaining 3 tablespoons of sugar and the lemon juice in a processor/blender. Process to a smooth purée, then pass through a fine sieve into a bowl to remove the skins. Refrigerate the sauce until it is chilled – about ½ an hour.

To unmould the cooled custards, run a small sharp knife round the inside of each ramekin. Invert a serving plate over the top and turn both over together. The custard should slip out easily. If it does not, rock the ramekin from side to side to loosen it. Ladle some of the plum sauce round each custard; sprinkle the toasted almonds over the top.

Lemon-Buttermilk Custards with Candied Lemon

Serves 8

Working time: about 20 minutes

Total time: about 2 hours and 40 minutes (includes chilling)

Calories 185

Protein 5g

Cholesterol 70mg

Total fat 2g

Saturated fat 1g

Sodium 115mg

2	eggs	**2**
200 g	caster sugar	**7 oz**
45 g	plain flour	**1½ oz**
2 tsp	pure lemon extract	**2 tsp**

¾ litre	buttermilk	**1¼ pints**
3	lemons, thinly sliced, for garnish	**3**
60 g	raspberries for garnish	**2 oz**

Preheat the oven to 150°C (300°F or Mark 2).

To prepare the custard, first whisk the eggs in a bowl, then whisk in 135 g (4½ oz) of the sugar and the flour; when the custard is smooth, stir in the lemon extract and buttermilk. Pour the custard into eight 12.5 cl (4 fl oz) ramekins and set them on a baking sheet. Bake the custards until they are puffed up and set, and a knife inserted at the edge comes out clean – 15 to 20 minutes. Let the custards cool slightly, then refrigerate them until they are well chilled – about 2 hours.

To make the candied lemon slices, lightly oil a baking sheet and set it aside. Combine the remaining sugar with 4 tablespoons of water in a small, heavy-bottomed saucepan. Bring the mixture to the boil, then reduce the heat to low and cook, stirring occasionally, until the sugar has dissolved and the syrup is clear – about 1½ minutes. Add the lemon slices to the pan; immediately turn the slices over, coating them well, and cook them for about 30 seconds. Transfer the slices to the oiled baking sheet.

To serve, run a small knife round the inside of each ramekin and invert the custards on to serving plates. Garnish each plate with a few candied lemon slices and a sprinkle of fresh raspberries.

Rice Pudding with Raspberry Sauce

Serves 8

Working time: about 50 minutes

Total time: about 3 hours

Calories
225
Protein
7g
Cholesterol
45mg
Total fat
3g
Saturated fat
2g
Sodium
140mg

litre	semi-skimmed milk	1¾ pints
▶ g	long-grain rice	3 oz
25 g	sugar	4 oz
tsp	salt	¼ tsp
	egg yolk	1
tbsp	plain flour	3 tbsp
tsp	grated nutmeg	½ tsp

1 tsp	pure vanilla extract	1 tsp
¼ tsp	almond extract	¼ tsp
45 g	sultanas	1½ oz
250 g	fresh or frozen whole raspberries, thawed	8 oz
	fresh mint leaves (optional)	

ring ¾ litre (1¼ pints) of the milk to the boil in heavy-bottomed saucepan over medium heat. reduce the heat to low and add the rice, 50 g ½ oz) of the sugar and the salt. Cook the ixture, stirring frequently, for 50 minutes.

To prepare the pastry cream, whisk together e egg yolk and 4 tablespoons of the remaining ilk. Whisk in the flour and 50 g (1½ oz) of the remaining sugar; then blend in the remaining ilk. Bring the mixture to the boil over medium eat, stirring constantly, then cook it, stirring gorously, for 2 minutes more. Remove the pan om the heat and stir in the nutmeg, and vanilla nd almond extracts.

When the rice has finished cooking, stir in the

sultanas, then fold in the pastry cream. Transfer the pudding to a clean bowl. To prevent a skin from forming on its surface, press a sheet of plastic film directly on to the pudding. Refrigerate the pudding until it is cold – about 2 hours.

To prepare the sauce, purée the raspberries and the remaining 25 g (1 oz) sugar in a blender or food processor. Rub the purée through a fine sieve with a plastic spatula or the back of a wooden spoon; discard the seeds.

To serve, divide the sauce among eight serving dishes. Top the sauce with individual scoops of pudding; if you like, sprinkle the scoops with some additional nutmeg and garnish each with a sprig of mint.

Maple Mousse with Glazed Apple Nuggets

Serves 6

Working
time: about
1 hour

Total time:
about
1 hour and
45 minutes

Calories
215

Protein
2g

Cholester
25mg

Total fat
7g

Saturated f
4g

Sodium
35mg

15 g	unsalted butter	½ oz	6 tbsp	double cream	6 tb
2	tart green apples, peeled, cored cut into 1 cm (½ inch) cubes	2	½ tsp	pure vanilla extract	½ t
1 tsp	fresh lemon juice	1 tsp	3	egg whites, at room temperature	
175 g	maple syrup	6 oz	5 tbsp	light brown sugar	5 tb

Melt the butter in a frying pan over medium-high heat. When hot, add the apple and lemon juice; sauté the cubes, turning frequently, until they are light brown – about 10 minutes. Dribble 1 tablespoon of the maple syrup over the apple and sauté for 1 minute more. Transfer the glazed apple to a plate and refrigerate.

In a bowl, whip the cream until it holds stiff peaks, stir in the vanilla, then refrigerate. Put the egg whites into a deep bowl and set them aside.

To prepare the maple flavouring, combine half of the remaining syrup and the sugar in a small pan. Bring to the boil and cook it to the soft-ball stage over medium heat. Begin testing after 4 minutes: with a spoon, drop a bit of syrup into a bowl filled with iced water. When it can be rolled into a ball, start beating the egg whites with an electric mixer on medium-high speed.

Pour the hot syrup into the whites in a th steady stream, beating as you pour. Continue beat the whites until the meringue has cooled room temperature – about 7 minutes. Gen fold the cream and the chilled apple pieces ir the meringue. (Do not overfold.) Immediate spoon the mousse into six individual dishes a refrigerate them for at least 45 minutes.

To prepare the maple sugar, bring t remaining syrup to the boil in a small pa Reduce the heat to medium and cook the syru stirring, until the mixture crystallizes – about minutes. Remove the pan from the heat a allow to cool for 10 minutes, stirring occasional Scrape the sugar out of the pan on to a wo surface. Crush the sugar until finely crumble

Just before serving, sprinkle some of t maple sugar on to each portion of mousse.

Orange and Buttermilk Parfaits

Serves 8

Working time: about 40 minutes

Total time: about 1 hour and 10 minutes

Calories
145

Protein
5g

Cholesterol
70mg

Total fat
2g

Saturated fat
1g

Sodium
75mg

5 cl	buttermilk	12 fl oz		4 tbsp	frozen orange juice concentrate, thawed	4 tbsp
tbsp	powdered gelatine	¼ tbsp		2	oranges, for garnish	2
50 g	sugar	5 oz				
	eggs, separated, plus 1 egg white	2				

Put ¼ litre (8 fl oz) of the buttermilk, gelatine, tbsp of sugar and egg yolks into a pan over low heat. Cook, stirring constantly, until it is thick enough to coat the back of a spoon – to 8 minutes. (Do not boil or the mixture will curdle.) Divide between two bowls. Whisk the remaining buttermilk into one of the bowls; whisk the orange juice into the other. Set aside at room temperature.

Make Italian meringue. Pour the egg whites into a bowl. With an electric mixer; start beating the egg whites as soon as the syrup is ready.

Heat the remaining sugar with 4 tbsp of water in a pan over medium-high heat. Boil until the water has nearly evaporated and the sugar itself is beginning to cook. With a spoon, drop a little of the syrup into iced water to test. When the syrup in the water can be rolled into a supple ball, start the mixer.

Begin beating the egg whites at high speed. Pour the syrup into the bowl in a thin, steady stream. When all the syrup has been incorporated, decrease the speed to medium; continue beating until the whites are glossy, have stiff peaks and have cooled to room temperature. Beat for 1 minute more at high speed.

Mix a few heaped spoonfuls of the meringue into each of the buttermilk mixtures. Fold half of the remaining meringue into each mixture.

Spoon the mixture containing the extra buttermilk into eight glasses and top it with the orange mixture. Refrigerate for at least 30 minutes.

For the garnish, segment the two oranges. Just before serving, garnish each portion with orange segments.

Raisin Cheesecake

Serves 12

Working
time: about
1 hour

Total time:
about
5 hours
(includes
chilling)

Calories
120

Protein
7g

Cholesterol
11mg

Total fat
3g

Saturated fat
2g

Sodium
150mg

45 g	sultanas	1½ oz	1 tsp	pure vanilla extract	1 tsp
45 g	raisins	1½ oz	100 g	caster sugar	3½ o
¼ litre	plain low-fat yogurt	8 fl oz	12.5 cl	semi-skimmed milk	4 fl oz
90 g	low-fat creamy soft cheese	3 oz	1 tbsp	powdered gelatine	1 tbsp
300 g	low-fat cottage cheese	10 oz	3	egg whites, at room temperature	

Put the sultanas and raisins in a bowl and add ¼ litre (8 fl oz) of hot water. Set aside.

Purée the yogurt, cheeses, vanilla and half the sugar in a processor/blender. Scrape into a large bowl.

Pour the milk into a pan. Sprinke the gelatine over the milk and let stand until it softens – about 5 minutes. Heat the milk over medium heat, stirring until the gelatine is dissolved. Stir into the cheese mixture and set it aside.

Put the egg whites into a bowl.

To prepare the meringue, heat the remaining sugar with 2 tbsp of water in a pan over medium-high heat. Boil until the bubbles surface in a random pattern, indicating the water has nearly evaporated and the sugar is begining to cook.

With a spoon, drop a little of the syrup into iced water. If it dissolves immediately, continue cooking the syrup. When the syrup in the water can be rolled into a supple ball, beat the egg whites with a mixer on high speed. Pour the syrup down the side of the bowl in a thin, steady stream. Once incorporated, decrease the speed to medium; beat until the whites are glossy, formed stiff peaks and cooled to room temperature – about 10 minutes. Beat for 1 minute more at high speed.

Line a 20 cm (8 inch) cake tin with plastic film. Drain the sultanas and raisins and scatter in the bottom of the tin. Mix about one third of the meringue into the cheese mixture. Gently fold in the rest of the meringue, pour the mixture into the lined tin. Chill for 4 hours.

To turn out, invert a plate on top of the tin then turn both over. Lift away the tin, peel off the plastic film, and slice the cheesecake for serving.

Marbled Angel Food Cake

Serves 12

Working time: about 25 minutes

Total time: about 2 hours and 30 minutes

Calories 130

Protein 4g

Cholesterol 0mg

Total fat 0g

Saturated fat 0g

Sodium 65mg

100 g	plain flour	3½ oz	1 tsp	cream of tartar	1 tsp
5 tbsp	unsweetened cocoa powder	3 tbsp	½ tsp	almond extract	½ tsp
250 g	caster sugar	8 oz	½ tsp	pure vanilla extract	½ tsp
½ tsp	salt	⅛ tsp	1 tbsp	icing sugar	1 tbsp
10	egg whites	10			

Sift 5 tablespoons of the flour, the cocoa powder and 2 tablespoons of the sugar into a bowl. Sift the cocoa mixture three more times and set the bowl aside. Sift the remaining flour, salt and 2 tablespoons of the remaining sugar into a second bowl. Sift this mixture three more times and set it aside too.

Preheat the oven to 180°C (350°F or Mark 4). Rinse out a tube cake tin and shake – do not wipe – it dry.

With an electric mixer, beat the egg whites until soft peaks form when the beater is lifted. Add the cream of tartar, then blend in the remaining sugar a little at a time, beating the egg whites until they form stiff peaks. With the mixer set on the lowest speed, blend in the almond extract, then the vanilla extract. Transfer half of the beaten egg whites to a clean bowl.

Fold the dry cocoa mixture into the beaten egg whites in one bowl, then pour this chocolate batter into the tube tin. Fold the remaining dry mixture into the beaten egg whites in the other bowl, and spoon the batter over the chocolate batter in the tube tin. Plunge a spatula down through both layers of batter, then bring it back to the surface with a twisting motion. Repeat this step at 2.5 cm (1 inch) intervals round the cake to marble the batter thoroughly.

Bake the cake for 45 minutes. Invert the tin and let the cake cool for 90 minutes. Run a knife round the sides of the tin to loosen the cake before turning it out. Sift the icing sugar over the cake.

Spiced Pumpkin Mousse with Lemon Cream

Serves 6

Working time: about 30 minutes

Total time: about 2 hours (includes chilling)

Calories 140

Protein 4g

Cholesterol 18mg

Total fat 5g

Saturated fat 3g

Sodium 90mg

2½ tsp	powdered gelatine	2½ tsp
6 tbsp	caster sugar	6 tbsp
2 tsp	grated lemon rind	2 tsp
¾ tsp	aniseeds, finely ground	¾ tsp
⅛ tsp	grated nutmeg	⅛ tsp
1 tbsp	finely chopped crystallized ginger	1 tbsp
⅛ tsp	salt	⅛ tsp
250 g	canned pumpkin	8 oz

4 tbsp	fresh lemon juice	4 tbsp
4	egg whites, at room temperature	4
⅛ tsp	cream of tartar	⅛ tsp
	Lemon Cream	
25 g	lemon rind, julienned	¾ oz
2 tbsp	caster sugar	2 tbsp
2 tbsp	fresh lemon juice	2 tbsp
6 tbsp	double cream	6 tbsp

Put 4 tbsp of cold water into a bowl, sprinkle in the gelatine. Let it soften for 5 minutes; pour in 4 tbsp of boiling water and stir to dissolve. Stir in the sugar, lemon rind, aniseeds, nutmeg, ginger, and salt. Add pumpkin and lemon juice, stir. Refrigerate, stirring occasionally, until it starts to gel – 30 minutes.

When the pumpkin mixture is ready, beat the egg whites with the cream of tartar until they form stiff peaks. Remove the pumpkin mixture from the refrigerator and whisk vigorously for 15 seconds. Stir in one third of the egg whites and combine them thoroughly, then fold in the remaining egg whites.

Divide the mousse into 6 portions, mounding each in the centre, and chill them for 1 to 6 hours.

Put the lemon rind in a small saucepan with 4 tbsp of water, the 2 tbsp of sugar and the 2 tbsp of lemon juice. Bring to the boil, then reduce the heat, simmer the mixture until it becomes a thick syrup – about 5 minutes. Strain into a small bowl, reserving the rind. Set half of the cooked rind aside; finely chop the rest.

Just before serving, whip the cream in a bowl. Fold in the syrup and the lemon rind. Garnish each mousse with a dollop of the lemon cream and a few strands of rind.

Indian Pudding with Buttermilk Cream

Serves 8

Working time: about 25 minutes

Total time: about 2 hours

Calories 230

Protein 8g

Cholesterol 13mg

Total fat 3g

Saturated fat 2g

Sodium 125mg

90 g	yellow cornmeal	3 oz
1 tsp	ground cinnamon	1 tsp
1 tsp	ground ginger	1 tsp
1 litre	semi-skimmed milk	1¾ pints
165 g	molasses	5½ oz
1 tsp	pure vanilla extract	1 tsp

Buttermilk Cream

2 tbsp	cornflour	2 tbsp
4 tbsp	sugar	4 tbsp
¼ litre	semi-skimmed milk	8 fl oz
¼ litre	buttermilk	8 fl oz
1 tsp	pure vanilla extract	1 tsp

Preheat the oven to 170°C (325°F or Mark 3).

Combine the cornmeal, cinnamon, ginger and ¼ litre (8 fl oz) of the milk in a heatproof bowl. Pour the remaining milk into a saucepan and bring it to the boil. Stirring constantly, pour the hot milk into the cornmeal mixture in a thin, steady stream.

Transfer the cornmeal mixture to the saucepan; stirring continuously, bring it to the boil. Reduce the heat to medium low and cook the mixture, stirring constantly, until it has the consistency of a thick sauce – about 3 minutes more. Stir in the molasses and the vanilla extract, then pour the cornmeal mixture into a baking dish, and bake

it until it sets – about 1 hour.

While the pudding is baking, make the buttermilk cream. Mix the cornflour and sugar in a small saucepan, then whisk in the semi-skimmed milk. Bring the mixture to the boil and cook it for 1 minute. Remove the pan from the heat and stir in the buttermilk and vanilla. Transfer the buttermilk cream to a bowl and chill it in the refrigerator.

Remove the pudding from the oven and allow it to cool at room temperature for about 45 minutes; just before serving, top the pudding with the chilled buttermilk cream.

Kugel with Dried Fruit

Serves 12

Working
time: about
35 minutes

Total time:
about
1 hour and
35 minutes

Calories
325

Protein
13g

Cholesterol
17mg

Total fat
6g

Saturated fat
3g

Sodium
230mg

250 g	dried wide egg noodles	8 oz
200 g	sugar	7 oz
500 g	low-fat cottage cheese	1 lb
250 g	curd cheese	8 oz
¼ litre	plain low-fat yogurt	8 fl oz
1 tsp	pure vanilla extract	1 tsp
2 tbsp	fresh lemon juice	2 tbsp
150 g	sultanas	5 oz
75 g	dried pears, diced	2½ oz
60 g	dried apples, diced	2 oz

75 g	dried stoned prunes, diced	2½ oz
2 tbsp	cornflour	2 tbsp
½ litre	semi-skimmed milk	16 fl oz
2 tbsp	dry breadcrumbs	2 tbsp
	Cinnamon Topping	
30 g	unsalted butter, softened	1 oz
60 g	dry breadcrumbs	2 oz
½ tsp	ground cinnamon	½ tsp
2 tbsp	sugar	2 tbsp

Add the noodles to 3 litres (5 pints) of boiling water. Start testing after 7 minutes and continue cooking until noodles are *al dente*. Drain and rinse under cold running water, then set aside.

Preheat the oven to 180°C (350°F or Mark 4). In a large bowl, mix together the sugar, cottage cheese, curd cheese, yogurt, vanilla extract, lemon juice, sultanas, pears, apples and prunes. Dissolve the cornflour in 12.5 cl (4 fl oz) of the milk. Stir the cornflour mixture and the remaining milk into the cheese mixture.

Stir the noodles together with the cheese mixture, coating them well. Lightly oil a non-reactive 23 by 33 cm (9 by 13 inch) baking dish and coat it with the two tablespoons of breadcrumbs. Transfer the noodles to the baking dish.

To make the cinnamon topping, mix together the butter, the breadcrumbs, the cinnamon and the sugar. Sprinkle the topping over the noodles, then cover the dish with foil, and bake it for 30 minutes. Remove the foil and bake the kugel until it is golden-brown – about 30 minutes more.

Apple Gateau

erves 8

Vorking
ne: about
minutes

tal time:
about
4 hours
ncludes
hilling)

Calories
200

Protein
4g

Cholesterol
5mg

Total fat
2g

Saturated fat
0g

Sodium
180mg

g	cooking apples, peeled, cored and sliced	2¼ lb	90 g	demerara sugar	3 oz
g	granulated sugar	3 oz	2 tsp	icing sugar	2 tsp
	lemons, rind finely grated, juice of 1 strained	2	1	small red apple, cored, halved, cut into thin slices and brushed with lemon juice to prevent discoloration	1
g	breadcrumbs	8 oz			
p	freshly ground cinnamon	2 tsp	150 g	thick Greek yogurt	5 oz

the cooking apples, granulated sugar, half grated lemon rind and the lemon juice in a ge saucepan. Cover with a tightly fitting lid and ok gently until the apples are soft and fluffy. ur the apples into a large nylon sieve, suspended r a bowl, to drain and cool.

Meanwhile, heat the oven to 200°C (400°F or rk 6). Mix the breadcrumbs with the cinnamon l demerara sugar; spread out in a thin layer on rge baking sheet. Brown them in the oven for minutes, stirring frequently with a fork to vent sticking.

educe the heat to 180°C (350°F or Mark 4). ntly oil a 20 cm (8 inch) springform tin, or se-baked cake tin; line the base with a round

of non-stick parchment paper. Spread one third of the crumbs in the bottom of the tin, then spread half of the cooked apples evenly over the crumbs. Add half the remaining crumbs and then the remaining apples. Sprinkle the rest of the crumbs evenly over the top, pressing down lightly. Bake for 35 minutes. Remove from the oven, cool, then refrigerate until cold.

Carefully transfer the gateau from the tin to a serving plate. Sift 1 teaspoon of the icing sugar over the top, and decorate with the red apple slices. Mix the yogurt with the remaining icing sugar and lemon rind, and serve in a separate dish.

Honey-Glazed Buttermilk Cake

Serves 16

Working time: about 30 minutes

Total time: about 2 hours and 30 minutes

Calories 310

Protein 6g

Choleste 10mg

Total fa 6g

Saturated 3g

Sodium 190mg

375 g	plain flour	**13 oz**
1 tsp	bicarbonate of soda	**1 tsp**
450 g	caster sugar	**15 oz**
60 g	unsalted butter, cut into 1 cm (½ inch) pats	**2 oz**
60 g	polyunsaturated margarine	**2 oz**
2 tsp	pure vanilla extract	**2 tsp**
35 cl	buttermilk	**12 fl oz**

4	egg whites	
1	lemon, grated rind only	
	Honey Glaze	
4 tbsp	sugar	**4 tb**
4 tbsp	buttermilk	**4 tb**
90 g	honey	**3**
½ tsp	pure vanilla extract	**½**

Grease a 3 litre (5 pint) kugelhopf mould and dust it with flour. Preheat the oven to 170°C (325°F or Mark 3).

Mix the dry ingredients in a bowl. With a mixer on the lowest speed, cut the butter in until the mixture resembles fine meal.

Stir together the vanilla, buttermilk and egg whites. Mix half of this liquid with the dry ingredients on medium-low speed for 1 minute. Add remaining liquid and mix in at medium speed for 1 minute more. Stir in the lemon rind.

Pour the batter into the mould. Bake until it begins to pull away from the sides of the mould and feels springy – about 55 minutes. Set aside to cool.

Mix the sugar, buttermilk and honey in a p Bring to the boil over medium heat, boili stirring occasionally, until it is a light cara colour and has thickened slightly – about minutes. (Although the buttermilk in the gl will separate at first, the subsequent cooking yield a well-blended sauce.)

Remove the pan from the heat; stir in vanilla and 1 tsp of water. Let it cool – th enough to cover the back of a spoon. Invert cooled cake on to a platter. Lift away the mo and pour the glaze over the cake, letting the gl run down the sides.

Orange-Beetroot Cake

Serves 16

Working time: about 1 hour

Total time: about 1 hour and 45 minutes

Calories
190

Protein
3g

Cholesterol
50mg

Total fat
6g

Saturated fat
1g

Sodium
115mg

5 g	sulatanas	1½ oz	3	eggs, separated, the whites at	3
5 g	raisins	1½ oz		room temperature	
litre	fresh orange juice	8 fl oz	6 tbsp	safflower oil	6 tbsp
00 g	plain flour	3½ oz	1 tbsp	grated orange rind	1 tbsp
0 g	wholemeal flour	3 oz	1 tsp	pure vanilla extract	1 tsp
tsp	bicarbonate of soda	1 tsp	75 g	dark brown sugar	2½ oz
tsp	salt	¼ tsp	6 tbsp	plain low-fat yogurt	6 tbsp
tsp	ground cinnamon	1 tsp	3	raw beetroots, peeled and grated	3
tsp	ground nutmeg	1 tsp	135 g	caster sugar	4½ oz

ut the sultanas, raisins and orange juice into a aucepan. Bring to the boil then simmer for minutes. Drain the fruit in a sieve set over nother pan; reserve the juice and set the fruit side. Return the juice to the heat and simmer it ntil only about 3 tbsp remain – 7 minutes or so.

Preheat the oven to 180°C (350°F or Mark 4). Lightly oil a 23 cm (9 inch) springform tin. ne the base with greaseproof paper, then ghtly oil the paper, and dust with flour.

Sift the flours, bicarbonate, salt, cinnamon nd nutmeg into a bowl. In a separate bowl hisk the egg yolks. Stir in 1 tbsp of the oil. Vhisking vigorously, blend in the remaining oil

a tbsp at a time. Whisk until it is emulsified. Stir the orange rind, vanilla extract, brown sugar, yogurt, beetroot, sultanas and raisins into the yolk mixture. Fold in the flour mixture.

Beat the egg whites until soft peaks form. Sprinkle in the caster sugar and beat for 1 minute more. Stir one quarter of the egg whites into the batter, gently fold the batter into the remaining egg whites. Pour into the tin.

Bake until a knife inserted in the centre comes out clean – 45 to 55 mins. Remove from the oven and cool for 10 mins. Reheat the orange juice and brush it over the top of the warm cake.

Cherry Puffs

Serves 12

Working time: about 1 hour and 10 minutes

Total time: about 2 hours

Calories 170

Protein 5g

Cholesterol 75mg

Total fat 7g

Saturated fat 2g

Sodium 80mg

750 g	sweet cherries, stoned	1½ lb
4	lemons, grated rind only	4
12.5 cl	fresh lemon juice	4 fl oz
2 tbsp	cornflour	2 tbsp
4 tbsp	kirsch	4 tbsp
17.5 cl	plain low-fat yogurt	6 fl oz
2 tbsp	caster sugar	2 tbsp

	Choux Paste	
30 g	unsalted butter	1 ●
2 tbsp	safflower oil	2 tbs
¼ tsp	salt	¼ ts
1 tsp	caster sugar	1 ts
150 g	plain flour	5 ●
3	eggs, plus 2 egg whites	

Mix the cherries, lemon rind and juice in a pan over medium-high heat. Bring to the boil, then simmer for 5 minutes. Mix the cornflour with the kirsch and stir into the cherry mixture. Cook, stirring, until it thickens – about 2 minutes. Set aside at room temperature.

Whisk together yogurt and sugar; refrigerate. Preheat the oven to 220°C (425°f or mark 7).

Mix the butter, oil, salt, sugar and ¼ litre (8 fl oz) of water in a pan. Bring to the boil over medium-high. When the butter melts, remove from the heat and stir in the flour. Return to the stove; cook, stirring, until it comes away from the pan.

Remove the pan from the heat once more and allow to cool for 2 minutes before adding eggs. Incorporate the eggs one at a time, beating well

to a smooth dough. In a separate bowl, whisk th egg whites until frothy; beat ¼ of the whites int the dough.

Spoon the dough into a piping bag with a 1 c (½ inch) plain nozzle. Pipe on to a lightly oile baking sheet in 12 mounting swirls about 5 c (2 inches) in diameter and 5 cm (2 inches) apar Bake the swirls until they puff up and a uniformly browned – about 25 minutes. Turn o the oven, prop the door ajar, and let the puffs d for 15 minutes. Transfer to a rack to cool.

To assemble the puffs, slice each in ha horizontally and spoon the cherry filling into th bottoms. Top each filling with a tbsp of th sweetened yogurt; replace the tops and serve

Tangerine Chiffon Cake with Lemon Glaze

Serves 16

Working time: about 30 minutes

Total time: about 3 hours (includes cooling)

Calories
200

Protein
3g

Cholesterol
70mg

Total fat
6g

Saturated fat
1g

Sodium
110mg

250 g	plain flour	**8 oz**
1 tbsp	baking powder	**1 tbsp**
4	eggs, separated, plus 3 egg whites	**4**
6 tbsp	safflower oil	**3**
265 g	caster sugar	**8¼ oz**
2½ tbsp	finely chopped tangerine rind or grated orange rind	**2½ tbsp**
¼ litre	strained tangerine juice or	**8 fl oz**

	orange juice, preferably fresh	
½ tsp	cream of tartar	**½ tsp**
	Lemon Glaze	
90 g	icing sugar	**3 oz**
1 tbsp	fresh lemon juice	**1 tbsp**
1 tbsp	grated lemon rind	**1 tbsp**
1 tbsp	soured cream	**1 tbsp**

Preheat the oven to 170°C (325°F or Mark 3).

Sift the flour and baking powder into a bowl. Whisk in the egg yolks, oil, 135 g (4½ oz) of the sugar, and the tangerine rind and juice, and mix thoroughly.

For the meringue, beat the whites and cream of tartar together until the whites hold stiff peaks. Add the remaining sugar 2 tablespoons at a time, beating until the whites are shiny and hold stiff peaks.

Stir one third of the meringue into the batter, then fold in the remaining meringue. Rinse a 25 cm (10 inch) kugelhopf mould or tube cake tin with water and shake it out so that only a few droplets remain. Spoon the batter into the mould

and bake for 50 minutes. Increase the temperature to 180°C (350°F or Mark 4) and continue baking until a skewer inserted in the thickest part comes out clean – 5 to 15 minutes.

Remove the cake from the oven and let rest for 10 minutes. Loosen it from the sides of the mould with a spatula and invert it on to a rack. Cool – about 1½ hours.

To prepare the lemon glaze, first sift the icing sugar into a small bowl, then stir in the lemon juice and rind. Continue stirring until a smooth paste results. Stir in the soured cream and pour the glaze over the cake, letting the excess cascade down the sides.

Papaya Porcupines with Coconut Quills

Makes
about 20
porcupines

Working
time: about
30 minutes

Total time:
about
45 minutes

Calories
50

Protein
1g

Cholesterol
0mg

Total fat
1g

Saturated fat
1g

Sodium
14mg

2	egg whites	2
2 tbsp	fresh lemon juice	2 tbsp
75 g	plain flour	2½ oz
6 tbsp	caster sugar	6 tbsp
60 g	shredded coconut	2 oz

| 1 | papaya (about 500 g/1 lb), peeled and cut into about 20 chunks |

Preheat the oven to 200°C (400°F or Mark 6).

Prepare the coating for the papaya: in a small bowl, thoroughly whisk the egg whites, lemon juice, flour and 2 tablespoons of the sugar. Set aside. Spread out the coconut on a sheet of greaseproof paper.

Toss the papaya pieces with the remaining sugar. Dip a piece of papaya into the coating, then hold the piece over the bowl and allow the excess coating to drip off. Roll the papaya piece in the coconut, then transfer it to a baking sheet. Repeat the process to coat the remaining pieces.

Bake the papaya porcupines until the coating has set and is lightly browned – about 15 minutes. Serve the papaya porcupines warm.

Greek Yogurt Flan

Serves 8

Working time: about 0 minutes

Total time: about 3 hours (includes chilling)

Calories
115

Protein
3g

Cholesterol
60mg

Total fat
3g

Saturated fat
1g

Sodium
40mg

	eggs	2	1	orange, finely grated rind only	1
	egg white	1	3 tbsp	orange juice mixed with	3 tbsp
g	caster sugar	3 oz		3 tbsp cointreau	
g	plain flour	3 oz	8	fresh ripe figs, each cut into	8
0 g	thick Greek yogurt	8 oz		8 pieces, skin removed if bitter	
bsp	sifted icing sugar	1 tbsp			

at the oven to 180°C (350°F or Mark 4). Butter 2 cm (10 inch) fluted sponge flan tin. Put the gs, egg white and sugar into a large bowl and epare the sponge mixture as follows. Beat the gs, egg white and sugar with a mixer for 6 to ninutes. The mixture should be creamy and l off the whisk in a thick ribbon. Sift the flour the top of the mixture, lightly tapping the le of the sieve with your hand. Using a rubber atula or large metal spoon, gently incorporate e flour by cutting and folding it into the xture. Lightly butter a fluted flan tin. Pour the xture into the prepared tin and spread it enly. Bake for 25 minutes, until very lightly

browned and springy to the touch. Turn out on to a wire rack to cool.

Put one third of the yogurt into a piping bag fitted with a star nozzle and refrigerate until needed. Mix the remaining yogurt with the icing sugar and the finely grated orange rind.

Place the sponge flan on a serving dish. Spoon the orange juice and cointreau evenly over the centre of the flan, then spread the orange-flavoured yogurt on top. Pipe a decorative border round the edge with the yogurt in the piping bag. Arrange the fig pieces on the yogurt in the centre. Cover loosely with plastic film and chill in the refrigerator for 1 hour before serving.

Strawberry Trifle Gateau

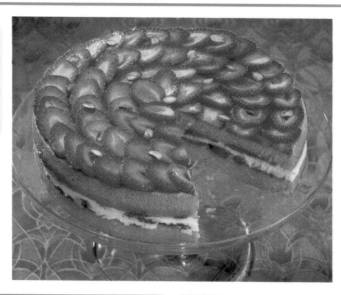

Serves 8

Working time: about 35 minutes

Total time: about 6 hours (includes chilling)

Calories 240

Protein 10g

Cholesterol 90mg

Total fat 3g

Saturated f 1g

Sodium 50mg

3	eggs	**3**
1	egg white	**1**
200 g	caster sugar	**7 oz**
125 g	plain flour	**4 oz**
750 g	fresh strawberries 500 g (1 lb) hulled and thinly sliced, the	**1½ lb**

	rest reserved for decoration	
250 g	quark	**8**
1 tsp	pure vanilla extract	**1**
1 tsp	icing sugar	**1**
15 g	shelled pistachio nuts, skinned and thinly sliced	**½**

Heat the oven to 180°C (350°F of Mark 4). Lightly oil a 22 cm (10 inch) springform tin or cake tin. Line the base with greaseproof paper.

Put the eggs and egg white into a bowl with 125 g (4 oz) of the caster sugar and beat with a mixer for 6 to 8 minutes. The mixture should be creamy and fall off the whisk in a thick ribbon. Sift the flour on the top of the mixture. Using a rubber spatula or large metal spoon, gently incorporate the flour. Lightly butter a fluted flan tin. Pour the mixture into the prepared tin and spread it evenly. Bake for 25 to 30 minutes, until pale gold and springy. Leave to cool in the tin for a few minutes, then carefully turn out on to a wire rack to cool completely.

Put the sliced strawberries into a bowl with

50 g (2 oz) of the caster sugar. Mix well, co and leave to stand for about 1½ hours. Blend quark with the remaining sugar and vanilla.

Cut the sponge in half horizontally. Place bottom layer on a plate. Fit an expanding ring order to retain the shape. Spoon half the slic strawberries and juice over the layer, th spread on the quark. Spoon the remaini strawberries on top. Place the second spon layer on top. Cover with plastic film and pu flat plate on top. Place weights on top . Refriger for 4 hours, or overnight.

Remove the ring. Slice the reserv strawberries, and use to decorate. Sift on icing sugar and sprinkle with pistachios. Se chilled.

Lemon Cornmeal Cake with Blueberry Sauce

Serves 10

Working
me: about
5 minutes

otal time:
about
hour and
0 minutes

Calories
215

Protein
4g

Cholesterol
68mg

Total fat
9g

Saturated fat
4g

Sodium
90mg

bsp	desiccated coconut	2 tbsp	12.5 cl	buttermilk	4 fl oz
0 g	caster sugar	3½ oz	1	lemon, grated rind and juice	1
g	blanched almonds	1 oz	60 g	unsalted butter	2 oz
5 g	cornmeal	4 oz	2	eggs	2
g	plain flour	2½ oz	300 g	blueberries	10 oz
tsp	baking powder	1½ tsp	⅛ tsp	ground cinnamon	⅛ tsp

eheat the oven to 180°C (350°F or Mark 4). Cut easproof paper to line the bottom and sides of 23 by 12.5 cm (9 by 5 inch) loaf tin.

Grind the coconut with 1 tablespoon of the gar in a blender/processor. Transfer to a small wl. Grind the almonds with 1 tablespoon of e remaining sugar in the blender/processor; d the almonds to the coconut, and set it aside.

Sift the cornmeal, flour and baking powder o a bowl. Combine the buttermilk, lemon rind d lemon juice in a measuring jug. Cream the tter and the remaining sugar in a bowl; the xture should be light and fluffy. Add the eggs, e at a time, to the butter and sugar, beating ell. Fold in the sifted ingredients and the

buttermilk alternately, a third at a time. When the batter is thoroughly mixed, stir in the ground coconut and almonds.

Spoon the batter into the loaf tin. Bake until a wooden toothpick inserted in the centre comes out clean – 30 to 40 minutes. Cool the tin on a rack for 10 to 15 minutes, then turn out on to the rack to cool.

Just before serving time, prepare the blueberry sauce. Combine the blueberries and cinnamon in a small, saucepan over medium heat. Cook the blueberries, stirring occasionally, until they pop and exude some of their juice – about 5 minutes. Serve the sauce warm – do not let it cool – with slices of cake.

Crêpes with Glazed Pears

Serves 4

Working time: about 1 hour

Total time: about 3 hours

Calories 305

Protein 5g

Cholesterc 80mg

Total fat 11g

Saturated f 3g

Sodium 70mg

3	ripe pears	3
1 tbsp	fresh lemon juice	1 tbsp
½ tsp	safflower oil	½ tsp
4 tbsp	Sauternes or other sweet white wine	4 tbsp
3 tbsp	honey	3 tbsp
15 g	unsalted butter	½ oz
	freshly. ground black pepper	
	Sauternes Crêpe Batter	
7 tbsp	plain flour	7 tbsp
	one-sixteenth teaspoon salt	
	freshly ground black pepper	
⅛ tsp	caster sugar	⅛ t
1	egg	
2 tbsp	Sauternes or other sweet white wine	2 tb
1½ tbsp	safflower oil	1½ tb
12.5 to 17.5 cl	semi-skimmed milk	4 6 fl

Whisk together the flour, salt, some pepper, sugar, egg, wine, oil and 12.5 cl (4 fl oz) of the milk. Whisking, pour in enough additional milk in a fine stream to thin the batter to the consistency of double cream. Cover and refrigerate for at least 2 hours.

Peel, core and slice the pears. Sprinkle with the lemon juice and set them aside.

Heat a crêpe pan or a 20 cm (8 inch) frying pan over medium-high heat. Pour in the ½ tsp of oil and spread over surface with a paper towel. Pour 2 to 3 tbsp of the batter into the hot pan and swirl to coat the bottom with a thin, even layer. Cook until the bottom is brown – about 30 secs – then turn the

crêpe over. Cook the second side until browr about 15 secs more – and slide onto a plate. It shou be paper thin; if not, stir a little more milk into t batter. Repeat to form 8 crêpes.

Fold a crêpe in half, then in thirds. Put 2 on ea of 4 plates, and set aside in a warm place.

Boil the wine and honey in a frying pan ov medium-high heat. Cook until syrupy – abou mins. Add the butter and pears, cook until bar tender and glazed – about 3 mins more.

Divide the pears among the 4 plates. Pc remaining syrup over each portion; grind pepp over all and serve.

Fruit-and-Nut-Filled Phyllo Roll

Serves 6

Working time: about 40 minutes

Total time: about 1 hour and 10 minutes

Calories 185
Protein 4g
Cholesterol 8mg
Total fat 6g
Saturated fat 2g
Sodium 2mg

1	egg white	1
60 g	low-fat ricotta cheese	2 oz
1	orange	1
1 tsp	grated lemon rind	1 tsp
¼ tsp	ground cinnamon	¼ tsp
⅛ tsp	grated nutmeg	⅛ tsp
⅛ tsp	ground allspice	⅛ tsp
⅛ tsp	salt	⅛ tsp
3 tbsp	coarsely chopped pecan nuts	3 tbsp
75 g	raisins	2½ oz
1 tbsp	pure maple syrup	1 tbsp
4 tbsp	caster sugar	4 tbsp
2	slices wholemeal bread, toasted	2
2	sheets frozen phyllo, thawed	2
15 g	unsalted butter, melted	½ oz

Mix together the egg white and ricotta. Remove the rind from the orange and reserve it. Discard the white pith. Working over a bowl, segment the orange, dropping the segments into the bowl. Squeeze the last drops of juice from the membranes into the bowl. Coarsely chop the rind and segments, and add them to the ricotta mixture with the juice that has collected. Stir in the lemon rind, cinnamon, nutmeg, allspice, salt, pecans, raisins, maple syrup and sugar. Cut the bread slices into cubes and mix them into the filling. Set aside.

Preheat the oven to 180°C (325°F or Mark 4). Lay one of the phyllo sheets on a piece of greaseproof paper slightly larger than the phyllo. Lightly brush the phyllo with some of the butter. Set the second sheet of phyllo squarely on top.

Spoon the filling down one of the longer sides of the double phyllo sheet, leaving about 4 cm (1½ inches) uncovered at both ends of the filling. Lift the edge of the greaseproof paper and roll the phyllo once round the filling. Continue rolling the phyllo and filling away from you to form a cylinder. Tuck under the two open ends and transfer to a lightly oiled baking sheet. Brush the top with the remaining butter and bake it until it is golden-brown – about 30 minutes. Cool, then slice it into serving rounds.

Berry-Filled Meringue Baskets

Serves 8

Working time: about 50 minutes

Total time: about 5 hours (includes drying)

Calories 150

Protein 4g

Cholesterol 5mg

Total fat 2g

Saturated fat 1g

Sodium 45mg

3	egg whites	**3**
200 g	caster sugar	**7 oz**
125 g	low-fat ricotta cheese	**4 oz**
4 tbsp	plain low-fat yogurt	**4 tbsp**

350 g	hulled, sliced strawberries	**12 oz**
150 g	blueberries, stemmed, picked over and rinsed	**5 oz**

Line a baking sheet with non-stick parchment paper or brown paper. Preheat the oven to 70°C (160°F or Mark $\frac{1}{4}$). If your oven does not have a setting this low, set it at its lowest. Keep the oven door propped open with a ball of crumpled foil.

To prepare the meringue, put the egg whites and sugar into a large, heatproof bowl. Set the bowl over a pan of simmering water, and stir the mixture with a whisk until the sugar has dissolved and the egg whites are hot – about 6 minutes. Remove the bowl from the heat. Using an electric mixer, beat the egg whites on medium-high speed until they form stiff peaks and have cooled to room temperature.

Transfer the meringue to a piping bag fitted with 1 cm ($\frac{1}{2}$ inch) nozzle. Holding the nozzle about 1 cm ($\frac{1}{2}$ inch) above the surface of the baking sheet, pipe out the meringue in a tightly coiled spiral until you have formed a flat disc about 8.5 cm ($3\frac{1}{2}$ inches) across. Pipe a single ring of meringue on top of the edge of the disc, forming a low wall that will hold in the filling. Form seven more meringue baskets in the same way.

Put the baking sheet into the oven and let the meringues bake for at least 4 hours. The meringues should remain white and be thoroughly dried out. Let the meringues stand at room temperature until they cool – they will become quite crisp.

Purée the ricotta with the yogurt in a food processor or a blender. Divide the cheese mixture among the meringue baskets, and top each with some of the strawberries and blueberries.

Rolled Cherry-Walnut Cake

Serves 8

Working time: about 1 hour

Total time: about 1 hour and 30 minutes

Calories
140
Protein
5g
Cholesterol
70mg
Total fat
4g
Saturated fat
1g
Sodium
70mg

)g	shelled walnuts, finely chopped	**1 oz**
½ tbsp	plain flour	**1½ tbsp**
tsp	baking powder	**½ tsp**
	eggs, separated, plus 1 egg white, the whites at room temperature	**2**
tbsp	dark brown sugar	**2 tbsp**
tsp	pure vanilla extract	**½ tsp**
tbsp	caster sugar	**4 tbsp**
2 tsp	icing sugar	**2 tsp**
	Cherry Filling	
½ tsp	pure vanilla extract	**½ tsp**
¼ litre	plain low-fat yogurt	**8 fl oz**
2 tbsp	caster sugar	**2 tbsp**
250 g	fresh cherries, stoned and quartered	**8 oz**

ot a baking sheet with butter. Line with reaseproof paper. Butter the paper, then dust ith flour and set the pan aside. Heat the oven ▸ 180°C (350°F or Mark 4).

Mix together the walnuts, flour and baking owder. Set aside.

Beat the 2 egg yolks with the brown sugar and ½ tbsp of hot water until it is thick – about 4 ins. Stir in the vanilla and set the bowl aside.

Beat the egg whites on medium until they form oft peaks. Increase to medium-high, gradually Iding the caster sugar, until stiff peaks form.

Stir about one quarter of the egg whites into e yolk mixture. Gently fold in remaining egg whites and nut-and-flour mixture, alternately, one third at a time.

Transfer to the baking sheet and form a rectangle about 28 x 18 cm (11 x 7 inches). Bake until golden and springy – about 20 mins. Cool – at least 30 mins.

Sprinkle a sheet of greaseproof with icing sugar and invert the cake on to the paper. Remove the baking paper. Stir the vanilla extract into the yogurt, spread this on to the cake. Sprinkle the caster sugar over the yogurt mixture, then scatter the cherries evenly on top. Starting on a long side, roll cake into a cylinder. Dust with icing sugar.

Useful weights and measures

Weight Equivalents

Avoirdupois		Metric
1 ounce	=	28.35 grams
1 pound	=	254.6 grams
2.3 pounds	=	1 kilogram

Liquid Measurements

$1/4$ pint	=	$1^1/2$ decilitres
$1/2$ pint	=	$1/4$ litre
scant 1 pint	=	$1/2$ litre
$1^3/4$ pints	=	1 litre
1 gallon	=	4.5 litres

Liquid Measures

1 pint	= 20 fl oz	= 32 tablespoons
$1/2$ pint	= 10 fl oz	= 16 tablespoons
$1/4$ pint	= 5 fl oz	= 8 tablespoons
$1/8$ pint	= $2^1/2$ fl oz	= 4 tablespoons
$1/16$ pint	= $1^1/4$ fl oz	= 2 tablespoons

Solid Measures

1 oz almonds, ground = $3^3/4$ level tablespoons

1 oz breadcrumbs fresh = 7 level tablespoons

1 oz butter, lard = 2 level tablespoons

1 oz cheese, grated = $3^1/2$ level tablespoons

1 oz cocoa = $2^3/4$ level tablespoons

1 oz desiccated coconut = $4^1/2$ tablespoons

1 oz cornflour = $2^1/2$ tablespoons

1 oz custard powder = $2^1/2$ tablespoons

1 oz curry powder and spices = 5 tablespoons

1 oz flour = 2 level tablespoons

1 oz rice, uncooked = $1^1/2$ tablespoons

1 oz sugar, caster and granulated = 2 tablespoons

1 oz icing sugar = $2^1/2$ tablespoons

1 oz yeast, granulated = 1 level tablespoon

American Measures

16 fl oz	=1 American pint
8 fl oz	=1 American standard cup
0.50 fl oz	=1 American tablespoon

(slightly smaller than British Standards Institute tablespoon)

0.16 fl oz	=1 American teaspoon

Australian Cup Measures

(Using the 8-liquid-ounce cup measure)

1 cup flour	4 oz
1 cup sugar (crystal or caster)	8 oz
1 cup icing sugar (free from lumps)	5 oz
1 cup shortening (butter, margarine)	8 oz
1 cup brown sugar (lightly packed)	4 oz
1 cup soft breadcrumbs	2 oz
1 cup dry breadcrumbs	3 oz
1 cup rice (uncooked)	6 oz
1 cup rice (cooked)	5 oz
1 cup mixed fruit	4 oz
1 cup grated cheese	4 oz
1 cup nuts (chopped)	4 oz
1 cup coconut	$2^1/2$ oz

Australian Spoon Measures

	level tablespoon
1 oz flour	2
1 oz sugar	$1^1/2$
1 oz icing sugar	2
1 oz shortening	1
1 oz honey	1
1 oz gelatine	2
1 oz cocoa	3
1 oz cornflour	$2^1/2$
1 oz custard powder	$2^1/2$

Australian Liquid Measures

(Using 8-liquid-ounce cup)

1 cup liquid	8 oz
$2^1/2$ cups liquid	20 oz (1 pint)
2 tablespoons liquid	1 oz
1 gill liquid	5 oz ($1/4$ pint)